The Concepts and Practices of Lifelong Learning

D0195404

It is difficult to overstate the significance of lifelong learning in contemporary society. *The Concepts and Practices of Lifelong Learning* gives a comprehensive, research-informed and multi-disciplinary introduction to issues in this field across a variety of educational settings and practices. In doing so, the authors present critical discussions within an international context.

Governmental, institutional and individual commitments to lifelong learning have brought changes in the meaning and significance of learning across the life course and new teaching and learning practices, as well as significant institutional change. The vision of the learning society that is unfolding is also highly contested. *The Concepts and Practices of Lifelong Learning* explores some of these contestations, meanings, practices and institutional changes.

Chapters cover:

- the various conceptions of lifelong learning;
- the factors that impinge on learning through the life course;
- the social and the economic rationale for lifelong learning;
- the varied sites of lifelong learning, from the micro to macro (from the home to the region to the virtual);
- turbulence and continuing transition in personal and work roles, and against the background of future technological development.

This timely overview will be relevant to education and training professionals in all education sectors, education studies students and the general reader.

Brenda Morgan-Klein is Senior Lecturer in Education at the University of Stirling, UK.

Michael Osborne is Professor of Adult and Lifelong Learning at the University of Glasgow, UK.

The Concepts and Practices of Lifelong Learning

Brenda Morgan-Klein and Michael Osborne

Routledge
Taylor & Francis Group

LONDON AND NEW YORK

First published 2007
by Routledge
2 Park Square, Milton Park, Abingdon, Oxon, OX14 4RN

Simultaneously published in the USA and Canada
by Routledge
270 Madison Ave, New York, NY 10016

*Routledge is an imprint of the Taylor & Francis Group,
an informa business*

Typeset in Galliard by
Integra Software Services Pvt. Ltd, Pondicherry, India
Printed and bound in Great Britain by
TJ International Ltd, Padstow, Cornwall

Every effort has been made to ensure that the advice and information in
this book is true and accurate at the time of going to press. However,
neither the publisher nor the authors can accept any legal responsibility
or liability for any errors or omissions that may be made. In the case of
drug administration, any medical procedure or the use of technical
equipment mentioned within this book, you are strongly advised to
consult the manufacturer's guidelines.

British Library Cataloguing in Publication Data
A catalogue record for this book is available from the British Library

Library of Congress Cataloging in Publication Data
Morgan-Klein, Brenda, 1959-
   The concepts and practices of lifelong learning / Brenda
Morgan-Klein and Michael Osborne.
      p. cm.
   ISBN-13: 978-0-415-42860-6 (hardback)
   ISBN-13: 978-0-415-42861-3 (pbk.)
   1. Continuing education. 2. Adult education. 3. Communities. I.
Osborne, Michael, 1954- II. Title.
   LC5215.M618 2007
   374--dc22

                              2007028587

ISBN10: 0-415-42860-2 (hbk)
ISBN10: 0-415-42861-0 (pbk)
ISBN10: 0-203-93276-5 (ebk)

ISBN13: 978-0-415-42860-6 (hbk)
ISBN13: 978-0-415-42861-3 (pbk)
ISBN13: 978-0-203-93276-6 (ebk)

Contents

Acknowledgements

We would like to thank colleagues at the Institute of Education, University of Stirling, for covering some of our work and responsibilities while we were on research leave. We also wish to thank Frank Stephen and Glen Postle for reading drafts of particular chapters and Lewis Morgan-Klein for editorial and proof reading help.

Chapter 1

Introduction

The scope of lifelong learning

It is difficult to overstate the significance of lifelong learning (LLL) in contemporary society. The scope of lifelong learning includes policies on and practices in schooling as well as adult education, and much besides including aspects of informal as well as formal learning across the life course. As a strategy, it is applied to aspects of social policy as in the encouragement of single parents to return to work or education and to interventions in families designed to raise the educational attainment of children. Moreover, educational institutions themselves have expanded their boundaries in many instances, as in community schools in Scotland and in England there are proposals to make some form of education and training compulsory for 16–18-year-olds who will face sanctions if they do not comply. Governmental, institutional and individual commitment to lifelong learning does not mean more of what we had before and has brought changes in the meaning and significance of learning across the life course, new teaching and learning practices and institutional change. The vision of the learning society that is unfolding is also increasingly contested. In this volume, we explore some of these contestations, meanings, practices and institutional changes.

It is clear then that lifelong learning is not simply a 'voguish' term for the activities associated with adult learning of various kinds. Indeed, some writers have sought to distinguish between lifelong learning and adult education indicating that 'lifelong learning' and the 'learning society' are contested concepts.

> What we need, paradoxically is less lifelong learning and more adult education aimed at increasing the individual and collective autonomy of communities. It is misleading to see the current fascination for lifelong learning as a more popular form of lifelong education. Something new and more pernicious is happening. (Crowther, 2004, 127)

Here Crowther is arguing that lifelong learning has little in common with previous 'visions' of the 'learning society' such as 'lifelong education' – a concept advocated by the United Nations Education, Science and Cultural Organisation

(UNESCO) in the 1970s and which entailed a focus on the provision of opportunities to learn throughout life including informal as well as formal learning rather than simply being focused on initial education. The concept of lifelong education is associated with social justice concerns particularly access to education and Crowther believes these concerns are missing in current lifelong learning practices.

The rather general focus of the UNESCO concept has been criticised as impractical and leading to little in the way of policy development.[1] It was not the only vision of that period, however. The Organisation for Economic Cooperation and Development (OECD) and the Council of Europe advocated the concept of 'recurrent education' in the same period. Recurrent education envisages regular participation across the life course in order to foster (mainly) career and skills development. This concept is related to human capital theory which emphasises the value of investing in education and training since this is assumed to bring returns in economic development and growth for individuals and also for society.

Lifelong learning, economy and politics

The current formulations of lifelong learning and the learning society originate in economic changes in Western democracies in the 1980s and in new directions in social and economic policies in the 1990s. Briefly, the 1980s were characterised by a renewed focus on the economic; partly as a result of the rise of neo-liberalism in Western politics and partly as a result of the effects of economic restructuring. The central tenets of neo-liberalism include a belief in the efficacy of free markets, competition, individual freedom and, crucially, a critical account of the public sector as largely a drag on economies and as inevitably characterised by inefficiencies. From this perspective, the role of the state should be strictly limited in order to ensure that the market is free to operate effectively.

Much of the political debate of the 1990s continued to focus on economic change and this was dominated by a concern that technological change in communications and production brought increased international competition. The challenge identified here is that of 'globalisation'. Globalisation is seen as particularly challenging because as distances shrink and information technology allows individuals and business to achieve more in given time frames, economic competition should sharpen significantly. Moreover, this implies the acceleration of everyday life and greater uncertainty in a global world where national governments have less control over multinational corporations. At the same time, and somewhat paradoxically, given the perceived threat of globalisation and the political legacy of the 1980s, the political rhetoric of the 1990s moved away from that of the 1980s. In the UK, for example, with the election of New Labour in 1997, there was a move to 'Third Way' politics. The nature of 'Third Wayism' and the extent to which it differs from the politics of the 1980s is contested. However, broadly it is concerned with the social dimensions of healthy and competitive societies including a concern with strong communities, equality of opportunity, individual responsibility and accountability. There is a reappraisal of the role of the state, a commitment to reform state services and a commitment to partnerships between the public and private sectors of various kinds – as opposed to simply expanding the public sector.

Lifelong learning as a strategy is first fully articulated in the European Commission White Paper *Towards the Learning Society*, published in 1995. This paper identifies the major challenges as the impact of the information society, the impact of internationalisation (or globalisation as it is commonly referred to) and the impact of the scientific and technical world. Also of concern is the problem of social exclusion in European societies. The White Paper suggested two main responses to these challenges including a focus on a broad base of knowledge and building employability in the new knowledge or information society. In addition, five general objectives were identified: encourage the acquisition of new knowledge; bring schools and the business sector closer together; combat exclusion; aim for proficiency in three community languages and treat capital investment and investment in training on an equal basis.

Towards the Learning Society is significant because it marked a turning point in the development of the idea and strategies of lifelong learning and the learning society. It was followed by a plethora of policy and strategy proposals at national level.[2] These had varying emphases across Europe. Common themes included the 'need' to respond to globalisation by improving employability and a focus on individual as well as state responsibility in achieving this. This meant upskilling and reskilling and therefore participation in education and training, but there was also a focus on the need for flexibility (adaptation to a changing workplace in terms of workplace practices as well as skills). In the preface to the English Green Paper *The Learning Age*, the new focus on learning is encapsulated by Tony Blair when he writes that '. . . education is the best economic policy we have' (DfEE, 1998).

The notion that learning throughout the life course is a good idea was not new in adult education circles but it became commonplace across society in the second half of the 1990s. As Field (2006) notes, the Cinderella status of adult education made this new emphasis and any new funding[3] associated with it attractive to the adult education sector. By 1999, a significant expansion of post- compulsory education and training was well underway in the UK and Coffield (1999) was able to write of a 'new consensus' on lifelong learning in the UK.[4] This consensus was characterised by a number of assumptions including the following:

- The idea that a nation's competitiveness depends on the skills of the labour force
- Globalization compels governments to respond
- Education as it stands cannot address these issues and must be modernized
- Individuals must take responsibility for 'upskilling'
- Educational institutions must become more efficient and responsive by following the model of British business (Coffield, 1999).

Coffield criticised many of these assumptions. He thought that the concentration on *human* capital ignored the relevance of other forms of capital including social capital[5] and that the economic models and models of change informing lifelong learning strategies were crude and questionable. They also deflected attention from more difficult issues such as inequality. Finally, he argued that lifelong learning policies may be seen as a form of social control because of the way in which they emphasise the need for individuals to adapt to change (as opposed to questioning the direction of change).

Reorganising education and training

It would be a mistake, however, to focus solely on economic issues such as the imperative to address the 'problem' of skills. Significant is the emphasis on individual responsibility and also individual choice[6] signalling a new relationship between the individual and the state characterised by an emphasis on individual agency and the state as empowering others (or, more minimally, extending choice) as opposed to providing services in all cases. Other aspects of social change are highlighted by Edwards and Usher (Edwards and Usher, 2000; Usher and Edwards, 2007), such as greater uncertainty, the advent of a post-traditional culture where there is greater plurality and uncertainty in all aspects of life (for example in patterns of family life), greater cultural diversity and greater heterogeneity of values.

These new diversities alongside the new emphasis on vocationalism in life-long learning strategies presented a particular challenge to the liberal framework of values that had characterised the educational establishment, including adult education.[7] This included a commitment to progressive sentiments (and, less often, practices) such as equality of opportunity and the notion of education as emancipating particularly where it is broadly defined. Lifelong learning by contrast is less clearly aligned to any one particular set of values. Indeed, Bagnall (2004) in an analysis of the ethics of lifelong learning has defined it as ethically promiscuous. What emerges here then is a picture of education at the turn of the century with the rug being pulled from beneath it (perhaps for good reasons depending on your point of view). In that sense one aspect of lifelong learning as strategy is the reorganisation of education and training. This has included, for example, expansion of tertiary education, diversification of institutions, restructuring of the academic year and courses of study in tertiary education, facilitation of adult learning, support for inter-institutional working between institutions and sectors, changes in funding regimes, comprehensive rethinking of learning in schools, greater focus on the individual as in personalised learning (PL) in schools, changes in governance at almost every level of the education system and so on.

Such changes are achieved in a variety of ways, for example by setting targets, adjusting funding regimes and other policy levers to particular ends and setting national standards and benchmarks as in National Qualification Frameworks

(NQFs) which regulate institutional curricula. We discuss aspects of these policy levers in this volume. Aside from such mechanistic devices, change whether of institutions or individuals is also realised and constructed in discourses embedded in policies and educational practices.

Reconstructing learners

One example of this is the way in which the concept of flexibility is deployed in ways that create imperatives for institutional and student action of various kinds. Institutions are expected to be more responsive and a positive notion of flexibility is constructed in 'responsive' activities such as the accreditation of prior learning. Here, a discourse of increasing global competition creates the 'necessity' of 'flexibility' which is constructed as emancipatory in practice, at least for students, and possibly also for teachers since it opens up the possibility of new types of practice. At the same time, the concept also creates a situation where students flexibly combine learning with work on their own responsibility, thus accelerating the pace of life and possibly intensifying teaching workloads. Moreover, as Nicoll (2006) points out, notions of responsiveness and flexibility are deployed in ways that promote institutional change such as the marketisation of education and training (since this may be argued to extend choice and responsiveness). Similarly, adjacent to the concept of responsiveness are the concepts of access and learner-centredness which are linked with humanistic notions of learning and social justice but which may also be deployed in ways that mean individuals manage themselves in ways that are aligned with particular lifelong learning strategies as we argue in Chapter 2.

The point here is that lifelong learning practices and discourses have wide social significance. So far, we have suggested that they are implicated in the shifting relationship between the state and the individual – some writers argue that the emphasis on individual responsibility in lifelong learning practices and policies is undermining the welfare state, for example (see Crowther, 2004). There is a renewed emphasis on the vocational and on markets and a questioning of old certainties such as the liberal framework of education. These are controversial ideas. Nevertheless, the imperative for change has led to the reorganisation of aspects of education and training often in the name of responsiveness and access. While these are seductive goals, individual and institutional changes inevitably reflect shifting power relations and possibly new patterns of inequality. In other words, they are not necessarily emancipatory even if they are effected in the name of learner-centredness or student access. These changes will involve the exercise of power and new types of surveillance for both learners and teachers. This is what Crowther is referring to as 'something new and pernicious'. We do not mean here that naked coercion is being exercised and encouragement to participate in education and training may of course bring positive benefits as we discuss in this book. Nevertheless, far-reaching changes in education and the meanings and discourses found in lifelong learning policies paint particular visions of the learning society. Inevitably, these are contested.

Visions of the learning society

A wide range of criticisms have been made of current moves towards a learning society. For example, there is a concern that there is too much emphasis on the vocational and the economic and not enough on the social benefits of learning and the relevance of informal learning.[8] This has led to a new interest in the social benefits of learning and a renewal of interest in the concept of social capital and its role in learning (Schuller *et al.*, 2004; Field, 2005). This perspective has been particularly influential and we discuss this in some detail in Chapter 3.

There is also criticism that lifelong learning policies and practices increase government control over individuals and institutions. These criticisms have been made from two main perspectives. First, there are those who wish to return to the social purpose tradition in adult education. Here education is seen as emancipatory only when it is broadly defined and linked critically with politics and political struggle. From this perspective lifelong learning is 'part of a hegemonic project to internalise compliance. . . . Learning to learn is part of the process of instilling self-discipline . . . ' (Crowther, 2004, 131–132).

Second, there are postmodernists who argue that lifelong learning is the post-modern condition of education. (Usher and Edwards, 2007). The argument here is that the current changes in education reflect the greater heterogeneity, diversity, uncertainty and fluidity of postmodernity. While these two perspectives are often presented as diametrically opposed, both are interested in changing patterns of control and power relations, for example Usher and Edwards are interested in '. . . the relationship between certain discourses of lifelong learning and changing exercises of power and forms of governing the social order' (2007, 170).

What these criticisms imply is that while it may be possible to identify the processes, practices and meanings of contemporary formulations of the learning society, these are contested and that there are potentially many visions of the learning society. In this volume, we explore the diversity of meanings and practices in lifelong learning.

In Chapter 2, we discuss learner identity and the ways in which this is socially shaped. Different theories about learning construct learners in particular ways and the chapter discusses the way in which explanations differ. It argues for an explicit focus on social aspects of identity and the relevance of identity and cultural capital is discussed. It is argued that lifelong learning discourses and practices help to construct particular identities such as the self-optimising entrepreneurial self. This raises the question of how individuals will resource these identities and indeed whether or not they are desirable.

Chapter 3 focuses on the social dimensions of lifelong learning. There has been increasing interest in the social benefits of learning and the discussion in this chapter reviews the debate on social capital theory considering some of the advantages and disadvantages of this approach. One of the key questions is the extent to which it is a resource that can be relatively easily accessed by the socially excluded and deployed by them to their advantage. The chapter argues that the ways in which we understand the social nature of learning are highly context-specific and the social purpose tradition in adult education is compared with social capital approaches.

In Chapter 4, we discuss the economic dimensions of lifelong learning and the way in which economic imperatives have been at the forefront of lifelong learning strategies and policies most notably in the Lisbon Strategy for the Council of the European Union. The chapter considers the perennial concern with skill deficits in the 'knowledge economy' and the economic costs and benefits of participation in learning throughout the life course for individuals and also for society.

Chapter 5 discusses the ways in which lifelong learning strategies and discourses are now applied to schooling and are driving particular changes. The chapter considers a number of key changes facing schools and examines personalised learning; greater connectedness between schools and a range of other stakeholders and partners and community schools. We conclude the chapter by considering possible future scenarios for schools in the learning society.

Chapter 6 discusses aspects of formal post-compulsory education. A key element of many governments' strategies for lifelong learning has been the expansion of participation in tertiary education and this has led to expansion and diversification of this sector. The chapter discusses differences between types of institutions and changes in student populations. In the UK, widening access to tertiary education has been a perennial feature of policy for some decades and we discuss the changing focus of policy over time and a range of different types of 'access' initiatives.

Chapter 7 considers the different dimensions of learning and work including learning for work, learning at work and learning through work. The first of these addresses the issue of skills for work and reviews some of the debates on the idea of 'generic skills'. It is argued that approaches that are too mechanistic may fail to consider other issues. Also discussed is the way in which the relationship between skills and gaining in work is complicated by other issues such as cultural capital for example the kind of university attended. The discussion of learning at work notes that economic benefits while tangible are not the only important factor in engaging learners in continuing professional development. The dimension of learning through work raises some of the challenges posed by accreditation of prior learning. Finally the chapter ends by examining some aspects of flexibility in work-related learning.

Chapter 8 discusses the social significance of informal learning. The chapter explores changing different governmental strategies such as formalisation of informal learning as well as renewed interest in the ways that informal learning may bring social benefits such as improved health and greater social cohesion particularly in deprived areas. A short discussion of the relevance of social capital in understanding family learning reveals some of the complexity within family processes. Finally, a brief overview of changing approaches to community learning demonstrates that this activity is highly socially specific and bound up with political change

Chapter 9 maps the contours of learning cities and learning regions. In such initiatives, social and economic imperatives are intertwined and involve a diverse range of actors and stakeholders. The discussion includes an overview of the different elements of learning communities drawing on a nested concept of learning environments.

We are told that developments in information and computing technologies are driving the need for lifelong learning and also that they can play an important part in delivering learning at all levels and across space and time. Chapter 10 considers some of the advantages and disadvantages of learning at a distance and also discusses the quality of the technologies available. Different generations of technology are mapped out as are a range of teaching and learning principles relevant to distance learning.

Notes

1 Indeed Field (2006) also argues that contemporary formulations of lifelong learning have failed to produce enough in the way of practical policies of implementation. Griffin (2000) argues that it may be more accurate to think of lifelong learning as a strategy rather than as a set of policies. In this way the role of government is to create the conditions for a learning society.
2 The first round of policy papers in the UK were published in 1998 and include *The Learning Age, Opportunity Scotland* and *Learning is for Everyone.*
3 The extent to which new funding was made available in the UK, at least initially, is disputed. As we note in Chapter 2, funding was withdrawn from certain types of adult learning in the mid-1990s and redirected.
4 He did not think this pertained uniformly across Europe and he thought that Trade Unions had been more influential in the direction of policy outside of the UK.
5 We discuss different forms of capital in detail in Chapters 2 and 3.
6 Choice is particularly evident in recent policies on schooling in England and on the emphasis on institutional flexibility (i.e. responsiveness to students, sometimes termed 'learner-centredness'). These themes are discussed in Chapters 2 and 3.
7 Clearly this is not the only set of values of significance and many adult educationalists would want to emphasis the relevance of a radical and oppositional approach to education. We discuss this in Chapter 3. Despite the intellectual and political significance of this tradition, we would argue that liberal values have predominated in British education.
8 There is evidence that this is changing and that there is currently greater emphasis on the social dimensions of learning as we discuss in Chapter 3.

References

Bagnall, R.G. (2004) *Cautionary Tales in the Ethics of Lifelong Learning Policy and Management: A book of fables.* London: Kluwer Academic Publishers.
Coffield, F. (1999) Breaking the consensus: Lifelong learning as social control. *British Educational Research Journal* 25(4): 479–499.

Crowther, J. (2004) 'In and against' lifelong learning: Flexibility and the corrosion of character. *International Journal of Lifelong Education* 23(2): 125–136.

Department for Education and Employment (DfEE) (1998) *The Learning Age*. London: HMSO.

Edwards, R. and Usher, R. (2000) *Globalisation and Pedagogy: Space Place and Identity*. London: Routledge.

European Commission (1995) *Teaching and Learning: Towards the Learning Society*. Luxembourg: Office for the Official Publications of the European Communities.

Field, J. (2005) *Social Capital and Lifelong Learning*. Bristol: Policy Press.

Field, J. (2006) *Lifelong Learning and the New Educational Order*. Stoke on Trent: Trentham Books.

Griffin, C. (2000) Lifelong learning: Policy, strategy, culture. Working Papers of the Global Colloquium on Supporting Lifelong Learning [online], Milton Keynes: The Open University, http://www.open.ac.uk/lifelong-learning (accessed January 2007).

Nicoll, K. (2006) *Flexibility and Lifelong Learning: Policy, Discourse and Politics*. London: Routledge.

Schuller, T., Hammond, C., Bassett-Grundy, A., Preston, J. and Bynner, J. (2004) *The Benefits of Learning: The Impact of Education on Health, Family Life and Social Capital*. London: Routledge.

Scottish Office (1998) *Opportunity Scotland*. Edinburgh: The Scottish Office.

Usher, R. and Edwards, R. (2007) *Lifelong Learning – Signs, Discourses, Practices*. Dordrecht: Springer.

Welsh Office (1998) *Learning is for Everyone*. Cardiff: HMSO.

Chapter 2

Learning through the life course

Introduction

In this chapter we focus on learners. However, this is not a discussion of the characteristics of 'typical' learners. Here we are concerned with aspects of learner identity and in particular the *social* nature of identity. First, we consider the way in which different learning theories offer different models of the learner. We distinguish between theories that focus on learners as individuals drawing on psychological or neuroscientific theories and those that consider learners and learning in social situations and social contexts. We then explore the relevance of learner identity and the concepts of cultural and identity capital to lifelong learning. We argue that lifelong learning discourses enjoin us to reconstitute our identities in new ways. These 'identity narratives' are controversial because they may be considered as empowering or regulatory depending on one's point of view. Moreover, learner identities constructed as 'desirable' in lifelong learning discourses are not necessarily available to all because identity is socially shaped and individuals are not free to situate themselves in any identity narrative they may choose.

Constructing learners in learning theory

The idea that learning takes place across the lifespan is not new in adult education. There has long been a concern with the particular proclivities and characteristics of adult learners.[1] These have been expressed in a range of learning theories. To take one example, 'experiential learning' theories emphasise the relevance of adult experience (see Colley, Hodkinson and Malcolm, 2003; Weil and McGill, 1989 on experiential learning). There is an almost bewildering number of typologies of pedagogical or andragogical approaches in the adult education literature (see Jarvis, Holford and Griffin, 1998 and Wenger, 1998 for useful overviews). We have resisted the temptation to overlay these typologies with our own tabular or diagrammatic formulations and nor do we propose to add to or provide an overview of the various typologies. Rather, our purpose here is to highlight the key differences of approach between theories, with a particular focus on the differences in the way that learners can be understood and to argue that social situation and social context are core elements in understanding learners. Nevertheless, we do begin with a simple descriptive typology which although not comprehensive (Boud, 1989, 40–43) provides a useful point of orientation and identifies four of the main traditions in adult learning:

1. Training and efficiency in learning
2. Self-Directed Learning and the Andragogy School
3. Learner-centred education and the humanistic educators
4. Critical Pedagogy and social action.

The first of these is centred on predefined tasks and goals and systematically organised learning. There is a degree of overlap between the second and third approaches, where the focus is on the *individual* learner. Boud highlights the concept of andragogy in the second – a concept popularised by Malcolm Knowles (Jarvis, Holford and Griffin, 1998; Smith, 2002) which emphasises the supposedly distinctive approaches adults have to learning. It draws on psychological notions of human development and stresses adults' experience, internal motivation, independence, autonomy and capacity for self-directedness. Similarly, humanistic approaches draw upon psychological concepts emphasising psychological needs, particularly the need for 'self-actualisation', which may be achieved in learning. Values such as personal freedom and the importance of learner autonomy are highlighted in such approaches, implying particular pedagogical approaches such as facilitation and group work as opposed to more didactic approaches. The fourth tradition diverges from the first three in that the focus moves from technical or psychological concerns to the social context within which learners find themselves. Here there is an emphasis on the purpose and politics of learning, and a concern with the way in which knowledge may be related to social relations of power in society.[2] Three different ways of viewing the learner are already evident from this very simple typology. In the first approach, the learner is objectified as the recipient of pragmatic education and training. The second and third present us with a principally psychological view of the learner and the fourth presents a more sociological account in which we see the learner in social context suggesting an interest in learners not just as 'learners' but as workers, parents, citizens and so on. These different 'traditions' do not only imply different understandings of the learner but also different pedagogic identities for adult educators, different ideas about the nature of knowledge and the relationship between theory and practice. Although we refer to these in passing in discussion, our principal focus here is on different learner identities that are partly constructed by theories about learning.

Technical answers? – Explaining learning

In a discussion which considers what a pedagogy for lifelong learning might look like, Zukas and Malcolm (2002) identify a range of pedagogic identities found across adult education and higher education. Three of these identities are relevant to our discussion: psycho-diagnostician and facilitator of learning; situated learner within a community of practice and critical practitioner. The first of these offers us a psychological model of the learner and a diagnostic, prescriptive model of pedagogy in which learners' learning styles and skills are to be diagnosed in order to discern appropriate teaching approaches. Usher and Edwards (2007) are critical of such an approach because it assumes that learning can be abstracted from social context in a technical and reductionist manner. Moreover, this diagnostic, prescriptive model implies an individualistic model of the learner that may overlook the *social* nature of identity and thus may present stereotypical or normative models of learners (models that are not sensitive to differences of class, gender or ethnicity for example). Theory is assumed to be developed in an *a priori* and technical manner and applied to practice. Zukas and Malcolm note that this approach has been most prevalent in the United States, though it is also influential in the UK and elsewhere. Such an approach can also be detected in the international debate about recent breakthroughs in the field of neuroscience and in particular the claims made by commentators regarding the implications of such new research for learning.

New knowledge about the brain is – potentially – highly relevant to lifelong learning across the life course. Two, perhaps quite obvious, questions arise from these new findings: the first concerns the effects of the aging brain on the ability to learn successfully and the second attempts to establish whether or not there are critical periods in the lifespan for particular kinds of learning – such as learning languages. A great deal of excitement has been generated by advances in neuroscience leading some to claim that it could lead to a new science of learning, 'Even though we still know relatively little about brain functioning, we know enough to bet on the fruitfulness of personalised learning with one way of getting started to be through a neuroscience-based understanding of education' (Spitzer, 2006, 61). We do know some useful things about the brain in relation to lifelong learning. However, it is worth beginning with a warning that this is a rapidly developing science. It would be rash to make premature predictions about the implications of recent research findings or future discoveries (though many do) and we have therefore refrained from doing so. Finally, our account is a highly simplified one, which avoids technical detail, interesting though that is.

Research has shown that learning is achieved through the growth of synaptic connections or the strengthening of existing connections in the brain (OECD, 2002). Since these connections continue to grow throughout the lifespan, then it is reasonable to assume that there is no biological impediment to lifelong learning. The brain's capacity to change over time is referred to as plasticity. The plasticity of the brain is popularly illustrated by the fact that the hippocampus (which stores information on spatial representation) is significantly larger in taxi drivers than non-taxi drivers, and the longer the period of taxi driving the larger the relative size (Hall, 2005). We accumulate synaptic connections throughout the lifespan; equally, we also appear to lose or prune some as part of new learning. This implies that experience is important and that it is possible that young and old may learn in different ways (Spitzer, 2006). It also highlights the connectivity and complexity of the brain. The separate structures of the brain do not operate in isolation and the popular idea of right or left hemisphere dominance is characterised by Hall (2005) as one of many 'neuromyths'. This complexity of function also implies that it is dangerous to rush into inferences about educational practices.

Different writers place different emphases on the issue of whether or not there are critical periods for learning. There is general agreement that the notion that the first few years of life are the most important has been overplayed, although most would agree that the period from birth until the early teens is critical for language acquisition (Hall, 2005). This could be taken to imply that the practice of delaying second language learning until the early teens may be misguided, although of course there may be other compelling reasons for doing so – student motivation for example. Again, the leap from neuroscientific insights to educational practices is clearly a long one. Finally, research has provided more information about the influence of emotional states on the brain and the way that this affects brain functioning. Negative emotional states appear to limit the capacity to lay down memories and to learn creatively (Spitzer, 2006).

What is the relevance of neuroscientific developments to our discussion of lifelong learning and what can we expect from the revolution in 'learning science' that is so confidently predicted? First, it is important to remind ourselves of the problematic nature of an approach according to which learning can simply be codified by either psychology or in the case of our example, neuroscience. If we consider the case of older learners in an aging society, it may be useful to have more neuroscientific expertise on brain functioning, but we also need to know about social aspects, such as social constructs of 'the elderly' who are often stereotyped in negative ways. Thus the issue of social identity will be important as will other aspects of social context – for example class inequalities in healthcare, which become particularly stark towards the end of the life course. Finally, there is something of an epistemological chasm when it comes to differences in theory formulation in the social and natural sciences, where quite different approaches are often taken in establishing what is 'known'. Some teachers might argue, for example, that they already 'knew' that negative emotional states were unhelpful for learning. This suggests that other kinds of evidence are relevant and perhaps that different models of theorising are in operation.

Participation and situated learning

Zukas and Malcolm's (2002) second model of 'pedagogic identity' – 'the educator as situated learner within a community of practice' contrasts with approaches drawing upon psychological theory. This model draws on Lave and Wenger's (1991) influential *social* theory of learning, which focuses on complex learning processes within 'communities of practice'. In this model, learning is not simply about the acquisition of knowledge in formal settings and nor does it focus only on internal processes. Rather, it involves informal and formal learning processes and encompasses engagement in a 'community'.[3] These communities are omnipresent and multiple, in that they are found at work, in families and so on. They generate ideas and meanings, shared understandings, a sense of belonging and offer learners particular identities. Therefore, this model demonstrates that we need to pay more attention to the social nature of learning situations and the social processes involved, rather than simply on formal pedagogy and content. For example, a student teacher on teaching practice will engage in informal learning which will include vital information on aspects of staff room politics as well as issues of classroom management. This approach emphasises participation and process, rather than the acquisition of knowledge: there is no sense in which this theory offers a set of learning theories which can simply be applied to practice; rather it stresses the significance and richness of social processes in learning situations. Here, identity is important and dynamic and is linked with a sense of belonging to a community, the meanings attached to that and to processes of becoming in learning (Wenger, 1998).

Understanding the learner in social context

An emphasis on the social context of learning looks beyond immediate learning situations and communities to wider issues of learner diversity, social identities and inequalities in education. It is impossible to overstate the significance of these issues in educational theory and there is a vast literature on social inequalities in both compulsory and post-compulsory education (see Archer, Hutchings and Ross, 2003; Ball, 2003; Cole, 2006 and Reay, 2006 for useful overviews). The relevant pedagogic identity here is that of critical practitioner which Zukas and Malcolm (2002) locate in various political traditions, including the social purpose tradition in adult education (see Chapter 3) and feminist critiques of curricula and of pedagogy (see Barr, 1999; Coats, 1994). Therefore the focus in this model is not simply on the ways in which socio-economic factors may inhibit participation, but on the ways in which learning situations and educational institutions may reproduce power relations, either through the content of curricula or by means of pedagogic practices which serve to actively exclude certain groups. Learner identity here is socially constituted and some identities may be more 'acceptable' than others. This model of the learner raises questions about social processes of inclusion and exclusion in education and their relationship to wider social divisions.

The relevance of identity

There has been a long-standing interest in the relevance of the social nature of 'learner identity' in education. In schooling, this has been most frequently expressed as a concern with the ways in which identities associated with particular social groups, for example social class, gender and ethnicity, either place children at a disadvantage in education or expose them to processes of exclusion within the education system (see Archer and Francis, 2005 and Osler and Vincent, 2003 for examples). Of relevance to these concerns with inequality and social exclusion are the resources individuals are able to draw upon when engaging in learning. Bourdieu (1997) originally expressed these as different forms of capital, including social and cultural as well as economic capital.[4] Social networks and relations are an important influence on and expression of identity. However, the concept of cultural capital is of particular relevance to an understanding of the importance of 'learner identity' for this discussion because of the way in which it is transmitted unconsciously as well as over time and as result can be read as the 'natural' characteristics and abilities of individuals. Bourdieu argued that cultural capital exists in three different forms or states: embodied, objectified and institutionalised forms. In the embodied state it includes particular dispositions of mind and body, such as accent, style of speech or style of dress. Objectified cultural capital refers to cultural 'goods' such as musical instruments, books and pictures. Institutionalised cultural capital consists of institutionalised cultural objects or goods in the form of educational qualifications. Most obviously, in certain instances, it will be important to display the 'right kind' of cultural capital such as in applying for a place at university or in writing a job application, but cultural capital is on display all of the time, particularly in its embodied state, and it affects learner engagement and learners' identities on a number of levels. Bourdieu proposed that '. . . ability or talent is itself the product of an investment of time and cultural capital . . . the scholastic yield from educational action depends on the cultural capital invested by the family' (1997, 48).

Crucially, at least for Bourdieu, the process of transmission of cultural capital within the family is linked to the amount of economic capital that the family is in possession of. This has been interpreted in various ways to mean that some socio-economic groups are culturally deprived; or that some types of cultural capital, such as middle-class values and certain types of cultural goods, for example being able to play a certain type of musical instrument, are valued in education more than other types of cultural capital. Both of these explanations suggest that particular social groups, such as working-class children or children from some ethnic minorities are at a disadvantage. Differences in cultural capital result in processes of social exclusion for specific social groups. These processes of exclusion are particularly powerful because they are seen to discriminate against individuals 'fairly' on the basis of 'individual deficits'. The important point of this analysis for our discussion of identity is that it suggests that identities are embedded in social and economic relations; that there is a hierarchy of value wherein some forms of cultural capital are regarded by some as being more 'useful' than others and that different social groups have differential access to the kinds of cultural capital that are most valued within the education system.[5] It has been suggested that one of the consequences of these differences in cultural capital is that some groups are more likely to feel comfortable in formal educational settings than others.

Identity capital and Social inclusion

In a somewhat similar vein, Schuller *et al.* (2004) has suggested that three forms of capital are important. These are human, social and identity capital:

> learning [is] a process whereby people build up – consciously or not – their assets in the shape of human, social and identity capital, and then benefit from the returns on the investment in the shape of better health, stronger social networks, enhanced family life, and so on. (p. 13)

Identity capital here is defined by individual characteristics such as '. . . ego strength, self esteem or internal locus of control' (Schuller *et al.*, 2004, 20). Schuller acknowledges that these personality characteristics are 'socially shaped'. Identity is highly gendered, for example (see Hughes, 2002; Skeggs, 2004). There are similarities here with Bourdieu's dispositional cultural capital in that the process of social shaping may actually be hidden from view and that the characteristics identified by Schuller read as the 'natural' characteristics of effica- cious learners or workers. The most significant aspect of Schuller's formulation, at least for the present discussion, is that identity capital represents a resource that individuals can continually draw upon when engaging in learning. At the same time, increased identity capital may also be an *outcome* of engagement in learning – for example, an increase in self-confidence. Moreover, the social nature of identity is highlighted by the prominence that Schuller gives to the interplay between the different forms of capital which he identifies, both in understanding participation and engagement in learning (or the lack thereof) and in identifying the benefits of learning. Crucially, Schuller observes that the farther along the life course learners are when engaging in learning, the more previous experience and accumulated capital is relevant in understanding participation and assessing the benefits of learning.

Schuller's account of identity capital emphasises the importance of learner experience in understanding the relevance of identity. Within adult education theory and practice, this is similar to the humanist focus on the uniqueness of individuals and the relevance and valuing of the individual adult experience found at the heart of andragogical approaches, as described above. However, it differs from andragogical accounts in the significance it accords to the idea that identities are embedded in social relations. There is a vast literature exploring the links between social relations and social structures and the way that these impact on learner identities. This relationship is often problematic for particular groups. Mature female students, for example, have been found to face partic- ular problems in reconciling aspects of care work in which they are engaged with participation in education and training (see Britton and Blaxter, 1999, for example). Some of these problems are essentially material, such as lack of time and money (La Valle and Finch, 1999; OECD, 2003), but these are mixed with issues of cultural capital or indeed, identity capital as defined by Schuller, or lack of knowledge, or, for working-class students, a sense that they are participating in a different, sometimes challenging, strange, or even hostile cultural milieu (Tett, 2000). Gallacher *et al.* (2002) found in their research on adult participation in further education that identity impacts powerfully on decisions to engage in learning, the shape of learning careers and contended that, at the same time, learning changes identities. They found that socially excluded adults often had discontinuous learning careers, and that they often found institutions culturally threatening, at least from the outside. Gallacher *et al.* characterise such individuals' learning identities as 'fragile' and dependent upon a number of social factors for success, such as having supportive social relationships, access to childcare, financial support, access to informal knowledge about an educational institution (for example knowing someone who had already attended that institution) and a supportive institutional environment.

Much of this literature arises from activities relating to widening participation in post-compulsory education and training to previously excluded groups and is oriented towards identifying the causes of non-participation. For Preece (2000), this sometimes means an unhelpful focus on the perceived deficits of individuals who need to be 'helped' or 'improved' in order to facilitate participation in education and the 'improvements' that this can bestow. As Preece points out, this sometimes directs attention away from issues of inequality. Moreover, the idea that participation necessarily offers 'improvement', 'self-actualisation' or 'emancipation' has become increasingly contested: some have questioned the increasing imperative placed on 'lifelong learning' as representing a narrowing and reactionary move towards learning for work (Coffield, 1999; Crowther, 2004; Martin, 2003). This charge is a central issue when considering lifelong learning policy, practice and as discourse (see Chapter 1). As Chappell *et al.* (2003) point out, education or learning is increasingly about changing ourselves. From a perspective that is critical of lifelong learning policies, practices and discourses, lifelong learning is concerned principally with changing our *working* identities.

New identities and lifelong learning

This emphasis on the need for personal change is found in discourses which emphasise acceleration in the pace of life, including the need for flexibility in the workplace, greater fluidity of career patterns and greater diversity of household composition and lifestyle. These changes in the pattern of the life course include social changes such as rising rates of divorce, falling rates of marriage, developments in reproductive technology and thus the proliferation of new family forms. We are expected to work 'harder and smarter' if we are to survive in a competitive, globalised world. Lifelong learning policies and institutional practices, such as diverse study modes and greater flexibility of education and training provision, reflect and reinforce a desire to respond to the challenge of change, which is identified principally in economic terms. Significantly, such discourses give a new urgency to the need for personal change in order that learners may adapt to the advent of a 'knowledge economy' and accelerated, more fluid patterns of production. Thus, the life course is represented as increasingly uncertain and challenging across a number of dimensions. [6] Edwards, Ranson and Strain (2002), for example, refer to 'Individualisation and detraditionalisation . . . anxiety over life trajectories . . . "pluralisation" of individual and collective identities . . . increased mobility around the globe . . . ' (p. 526).

There is thus a new emphasis on the subjectivities of learners which is often expressed as learner-centredness.[7] Yet this is not the learner-centredness of humanistic andragogical approaches to learning, because the aims of participation in learning are increasingly externally imposed according to lifelong learning agendas (Edwards and Usher, 2000; Usher and Edwards, 2007). Instead there is an emphasis on *performance* and most importantly an impulse towards the construction of new identities that can 'perform better' (Chappell *et al.*, 2003, 3). These new identities are attractive to individuals because they are represented as a way of coping with the insecurities of modern (particularly working) life and therefore as empowering. They are discursively constructed in policy, research and practice and accentuate individual responsibility, greater individual flexibility, entrepreneurship, 'creativity' and 'autonomy'. These, in turn, demand self-optimising practices including, most obviously, engagement in formal education and training. However, the emphasis on performance also spills over into informal learning, including activities designed to optimise the self, such as taking care of bodies, minds and relationships by joining a gym, regulating one's diet or reading self-help manuals. Skeggs (2004) characterises such activities as a form of utilitarian pleasure. Thus in lifelong learning discourses the optimising self is entrepreneurial; makes responsible choices which are adaptive to new working practices and comprise a new attentiveness to individual responsibility as opposed to relying on state provision. Crowther (2004) argues on this basis that, far from being empowering, this focus on individual subjectivity and identity in lifelong learning has a regulatory function:

> Lifelong learning is shifting the responsibility for learning to individuals, undermining welfare, disguising the reduction of the democratic public sphere, and working on people as objects of policy to ensure their compliance with the brave new world of flexible capitalism. (p. 130)

For Skeggs, the emphasis on utility and self-optimisation alters social relations in such a way that communication becomes increasingly strategic (for example as in 'networking' in business) and enlightened self-interest (behaving 'strategically') replaces integrity (see also Bagnall, 2004). For Chappell *et al.* (2003) the emphasis on a new learner-centredness and personal change in lifelong learning is internalised and this implies self-regulation and the potential for learners to be co-opted into '. . . managing themselves in line with both organisational and educational requirements' (p. 24).

In summary, we have argued that learner identities are socially constituted. They are constructed in learners' social milieux, in educational theories which offer different models of the learner and, importantly, in lifelong learning discourses. These discourses offer a prescriptive individualism with an emphasis on self-optimising and self-managing practices. Individuals are enjoined to participate in learning across the life course as a means of adapting to social and economic change. Therefore, lifelong learning discourses 'invite' individuals to identify with new identity narratives.

Identity narratives and identity politics

Field and Malcolm note that there has been a move away from consideration of issues such as social class in the adult education literature towards a focus on biography and narrative.[8] This may reflect both the contemporary individualisation of learning and the cultural and linguistic turn in social theorising – that is, a focus on the importance of meaning and discourse in explaining social relations (Field and Malcolm, 2006). It may also reflect the growth of what Ferudi (2004) calls therapeutic culture, which he identifies as an increasing tendency in contemporary Anglo-American societies to explain social phenomena in terms of their perceived emotional impact. He argues that this has led to a failure of the sociological imagination[9] and an intellectual life that is increasingly pre-occupied with the self. Here we are concerned not simply with individual identity narratives but with their relationship to wider social narratives. Chappell *et al.* (2003) argue that a narrative notion of identity '. . . suggests that a person's identity is created through its location and identification within social narratives that are not of that person's making' (p. 51).

These social narratives such as notions of the 'self-optimising entrepreneurial self' found in lifelong learning discourses may be empowering or regulatory according to one's point of view. In addition, and crucially, the ability of individuals either to adopt or resist such narratives will depend on the *resources* to which they have access. We have already noted that certain resources such as cultural or identity capital may be unevenly distributed. Particular identity narratives, therefore, are not equally available to all. We cannot simply choose to adopt any identity. This is illustrated by Odih (1999), who notes that contemporary ideas about femininity emphasise women's identities as relational (including taking responsibility for others' needs) rather than individualistic – that is to say that their caring responsibilities may mean that their sense of agency, for example control over time, are mediated through the needs of others. This may also be true of men in caring roles.[10] Moreover, we experience our care needs in different ways according to the resources we have in ensuring that these are met – or perhaps not met at all (Ehrenreich and Hochschild, 2003; Hughes, 2002). The constitution of identities in caring relations is of increasing relevance in an aging society in which traditional family relationships are in decline. Individuals' relationships to care and caring may seem a diversion from lifelong learning, but the point here is that care and caring imperatives and the identities constituted by them take us some way from the enlightened self-interest of the entrepreneurial self. We are here confronted with an important way in which identity capital is socially shaped. Caring relations are highly political in that they are gendered and vary across social classes. They are central to 'doing' the life course but they are ignored in the individualistic models of the self so prevalent in lifelong learning discourses.[11]

Concluding remarks

Crucially, the question of caring imperatives raises the issue of the identity, cultural and economic resources available to individuals in resourcing particular identity narratives. Also relevant is the relationship between such caring imperatives and the generation and availability of social capital (see Chapter 3). These resources are unevenly distributed, which means that some groups have greater freedom to choose how to situate themselves within different identity narratives prevalent within lifelong learning discourses – play the game if you like – or indeed to resist them successfully. The vital point is that identity is politically and historically situated. This has long been recognised throughout a wide spectrum of the literature on adult education, from the social purpose tradition (Crowther, 2004) to notions of the reflexive self.[12] However, the emphasis on the imperative for *personal* change in lifelong learning discourses obscures the *social* nature of identity, partly through its individualism and partly by its incorporation of the humanistic terminology of 'learner-centredness'. Discourses of lifelong learning construct the learner in particular ways that serve to reconstitute identities. This raises the political question of whether or not such identities are desirable. Moreover, social inequalities mean that different social groups will have differential access to the resources needed to situate themselves within identity narratives considered desirable in the contemporary workplace and in lifelong learning contexts.

Notes

1 These are sometimes presented as fundamentally different to children's. However, this is usually from a normative perspective on children's learning which ignores children's agency and the variety of social roles that children have and presents them as highly dependent learners.
2 See Chapter 2 for more on this tradition.
3 We discuss informal learning in Chapter 8 and aspects of learning in communities in Chapters 9 and 10.
4 We explore the ways in which the concept of social capital has been used in explaining adult engagement in learning in Chapter 3.
5 One aspect of this which is perhaps underexplored is the differences between institutions and sectors in education in the kinds of cultural capital that may be valued. This is perhaps most evident in the now-diversified university sector in the UK.
6 It is worth noting briefly at this point that the emphasis on accelerated lifestyles, hyper-mobility, increased risk and uncertainty are not without problems. In particular, some writers (see, for example, Skeggs, 2004 and Massey, 1994) have questioned the extent to which this reflects the experience of *all* social classes. As Massey points out,

mobility for some still means waiting at bus stops for buses that 'never come'. The main criticism here is that these accounts of hyper-mobility reflect the (middle-class) experience of the writers and that mobility is over-hyped. Similarly, flexibility and acceleration are also experienced differently by different social groups.

7　It is perhaps worth clarifying a range of concepts in popular use that relate to learners' learning pathways and narratives. The term 'learning career' has been popularised by amongst others Bloomer and Hodkinson (2000) and refers to events, activities and interpretations that develop individual learning dispositions over time. Learning trajectories refer to pathways that individuals negotiate through their life course, and because some individuals and groups are better positioned that others to take advantage of opportunity, their trajectories differ. For this reason Gorard, Rees and Fevre (1999) argue, for example, that men and women have different learning trajectories, and such differences are to a large extent determined by environmental factors at an early age. Thus self-directedness, which in one interpretation may be understood as the pre-disposition to take personal responsibility for determining ones own learning career and trajectory (see Brockett and Hiemstra 1991; Candy 1991), has to be balanced against personal circumstance.

8　This contrasts with the fact that Field and Malcolm found 'class' to be a meaningful category for individuals interviewed in their research project *Learning Lives.*

9　The concept of the sociological imagination was first outlined by the American sociologist C. Wright Mills in 1959. Mills (1970) argued that we often see social phenomena in terms of personal troubles rather than public issues. For example, we might experience unemployment as somehow a personal problem unrelated to wider economic factors. The sociological imagination allows us to make the links between personal troubles and public issues. Ferudi (2004) is arguing that therapeutic culture reduces public issues to private troubles by concentrating on the emotional content alone.

10　Odih in fact locates men in a more purposive instrumental rationality and responsibility for care of course remains highly gendered. One of us has written on this elsewhere, see Morgan-Klein, 2003.

11　Such considerations are also absent from many contemporary theories of the self.

12　Edwards, Ranson and Strain define this as the '. . . capacity to develop critical awareness of the assumptions that underlie practices . . .' (2002, 533). This implies self-questioning and questioning of the way in which identities are being reconstituted within lifelong learning discourses.

References

Archer, L. and Francis, B. (2005) 'They never go off the rails like the other groups': Teachers' constructions of British-Chinese pupils' gender identities and approaches to learning. *British Journal of Sociology of Education* 26(2): 165–182.

Archer, L., Hutchings, M. and Ross, A. (2003) *Higher Education and Social Class: Issues of Exclusion and Inclusion.* London: RoutledgeFalmer.

Bagnall, R.G. (2004) *Cautionary Tales in the Ethics of Lifelong Learning Policy and Management: A book of fables.* London: Kluwer Academic Publishers.

Ball, S. (2003) *Class Strategies and the Education Market: The Middle Classes and Social Advantage.* London: Routledge.

Barr, J. (1999) *Liberating Knowledge: Research, Feminism and Adult Education.* Leicester: NIACE

Boud, D. (1989) Some competing traditions in experiential learning. In Weil, S.W. and McGill, I. (eds) *Making Sense of Experiential Learning: Diversity in Theory and Practice.* Buckingham: Society for Research into Higher Education and Open University Press.

Bourdieu, P. (1997) The forms of capital. In Halsey, A. *et al.* (eds) *Education: Culture, Economy, and Society*. Oxford: Oxford University Press.

Bloomer, M. and Hodkinson, P. (2000) Learning careers: Continuity and change in young people's dispositions to learning. *British Educational Research Journal* 26(5): 583–597.

Britton, C. and Blaxter, A. (1999) Becoming a mature student: Gendered narratives of the self. *Gender and Education* 11(2): 179–193.

Brockett, R.G. and Hiemstra, R. (1991) *Self-Direction in Adult Learning. Perspectives on Theory, Research and Practice*. London: Routledge.

Candy, P.C. (1991) *Self-direction for Lifelong Learning: A Comprehensive Guide to Theory and Practice*. San Francisco: Jossey-Bass.

Chappell, C., Rhodes, C., Solomon, N., Tennant, M. and Yates, L. (2003) *Reconstructing the Lifelong Learner: Pedagogy and Identity in Individual, Organisational and Social Change*. London: RoutledgeFalmer.

Coats, M. (1994) *Women's Education*. Buckingham: Society for Research in Higher Education and Open University Press.

Coffield, F. (1999) Breaking the consensus: lifelong learning as social control. *British Educational Research Journal* 25(4): 479–499.

Cole, M. (ed.) (2006) *Education Equality and Human Rights: Issues of Gender, 'Race', Sexuality, Disability and Social Class*, 2nd Edition. London: Routledge.

Colley, H., Hodkinson, P. and Malcolm, J. (2003) *Informality and formality in learning*. A Report for the Learning and Skills Research Centre. London: Learning and Skills Development Agency.

Crowther, J. (2004) 'In and Against' lifelong learning: Flexibility and the corrosion of character. *International Journal of Lifelong Education* 23(2): 125–136.

Edwards, R. and Usher, R. (2000) *Globalisation and Pedagogy: Space, Place and Identity*. London: RoutledgeFalmer.

Edwards, R., Ranson, S. and Strain, M. (2002) Reflexivity: Towards a Theory of Lifelong Learning. *International Journal of Lifelong Education* 21(6): 525–536.

Ehrenreich, B. and Hochschild, A. (eds) (2003) *Global Woman: Nannies, Maids and Sex Workers in the New Economy*. London: Granta Books.

Ferudi, F. (2004) *Therapy Culture: Cultivating Vulnerability in an Uncertain Age*. London: Routledge.

Field, J. and Malcolm, I. (2006) Working identities: Gender, agency and social class. In Adair, N. *et al.* (eds) *The Significance of Agency on Lifelong Learning*. Symposium Presented at the 36th Annual Conference of the Standing Conference on University Teaching and Research on the Education of Adults, 4–7 July, University of Leeds.

Gallacher, J., Crossan, B., Field, J. and Merrill, B. (2002) Learning careers and the social space: Exploring the fragile identities of adult returners in the new further education. *International Journal of Lifelong Education* 12(6): 493–509.

Gorard, S., Rees, G. and Fevre, R. (1999). Two dimensions of time: The changing social context of lifelong learning. *Studies in the Education of Adults* 31(1): 35–48.

Hall, J. (2005) *Neuroscience and Education: A Review of the Contribution of Brain Science to Teaching and Learning*. Research Report 121. Glasgow: SCRE.

Hughes, C. (2002) *Women's Contemporary Lives*. London: Routledge.

Jarvis, P., Holford, J. and Griffin, C. (1998) *The Theory and Practice of Learning*. London: Kogan Page.

La Valle, I. and Finch, S. (1999) *Pathways in Adult Learning Research Report RR137*. Norwich: Department for Education and Employment.

Lave, J. and Wenger, E. (1991) *Situated Learning: Legitimate Peripheral Participation*. Cambridge: Cambridge University Press.

Martin, I. (2003) Adult education, lifelong learning and citizenship: Some ifs and buts. *International Journal of Lifelong Education* 22(6): 566–579.

Massey, D. (1994) *Space, Place and Gender*. Cambridge: Polity Press.

Mills, C.W. (1970) *The Sociological Imagination*. Harmondsworth: Pelican.

Morgan-Klein, B. (2003) Spatial and temporal issues in participation in higher education. Unpublished paper. Edinburgh: British Education Research Association (BERA) Conference.

Odih, P. (1999) Gendered time in the age of deconstruction. *Time and Society* 8(1): 9–38.

Organisation for Economic Co-operation and Development (OECD) (2002) *Understanding the Brain: Towards a New Learning Science*. Paris: OECD.

Organisation for Economic Co-operation and Development (OECD) (2003) *Beyond Rhetoric: Adult Learning Policies and Practices*. Paris: OECD.

Osler, V. and Vincent, J. (2003) *Girls and Exclusion*. London: Routledge.

Preece, J. (2000) *Challenging the discourses of inclusion and exclusion with off limits curricula*. Paper Prepared for Open University/University of East London Global Colloquium on Lifelong Learning, http://www.open.ac.uk/lifelong-learning/ (accessed May 2007).

Reay, D. (2006) The zombie stalking English schools: Social class and educational inequality. *British Journal of Educational Studies* 54(3): 288–307.

Schuller, T., Hammond, C., Bassett-Grundy, A., Preston, J. and Bynner, J. (2004) *The Benefits of Learning, The Impact of Education on Health, Family Life and Social Capital*. London: Routledge.

Skeggs, B. (2004) *Class, Self, Culture*. London: Routledge.

Smith, M.K. (2002) Malcolm Knowles, informal adult education, self-direction and andragogy. *The Encyclopaedia of Informal Education*, http://www.infed.org/thinkers/et-knowl.htm (accessed March 2007).

Spitzer, M. (2006) Brain research and learning over the life cycle. *Personalising Education*. Paris: OECD/CERI.

Tett, L. (2000) 'I'm working class and proud of it' – Gendered experiences of non-traditional participants in higher education. *Gender and Education* 12(2): 183–194.

Usher, R. and Edwards, R. (2007) *Lifelong Learning – Signs, Discourses, Practices*. Dordrecht: Springer.

Weil, S. W. and McGill, I. (eds) (1989) *Making Sense of Experiential Learning*. Buckingham: The Society for Research into Higher Education and Open University Press.

Wenger, E. (1998) *Communities of Practice: Learning, Meaning and Identity*. Cambridge: Cambridge University Press.

Zukas, M. and Malcolm, J. (2002) Pedagogies for lifelong learning: Building bridges or building walls? In Harrison, R. *et al.* (eds) *Supporting Lifelong Learning: Volume One Perspectives on Learning*. London: RoutledgeFalmer and the Open University Press.

Chapter 3

The social dimensions of learning

Introduction

In 2003 the OECD published survey data on adult participation in learning (OECD, 2003)[1] collected over nine countries.[2] These data form part of a thematic review which covers policies and provision as well as aspects of participation. The participation data make depressing reading, revealing entrenched inequalities in participation rates between different socio-economic groups. Briefly, the data show that amongst younger adults it is those with the highest educational attainment and in the highest skilled occupations who are most likely to participate in adult learning. Employers are reluctant to invest in learning and when they do, they are most likely to invest in high-level professional upgrading. Echoing other research (see, for example, La Valle and Finch, 1999 and St Clair, 2006) the review found that significant barriers to participation remain, particularly time constraints and lack of the necessary finance as well as a general lack of awareness, particularly amongst socially excluded groups. Similarly, despite policies to increase and widen access to higher education in the UK, there is continuing evidence of class inequalities, with the lowest socio-economic groups failing to increase participation rates significantly.[3]

We discuss the issue of access to higher education more fully in Chapter 6. Such inequalities are familiar and long standing. The point we wish to emphasise here is that these inequalities are extremely persistent in spite of significant changes in provision and the development of policies for a 'learning society' across Europe. This has led to a renewed interest, both governmental and academic, in a wider range of factors relevant to participation. Moreover, along with these concerns about the relative failure to include those from the lowest socio-economic groups, by the end of the 1990s, there was growing criticism of lifelong learning policies as simply too economistic and therefore unable to deliver greater social inclusion or indeed greater social cohesion. This prompted a renewed concern with the *social* benefits of lifelong learning arising from, '. . . a revalorization of social relationships in political discourse, after a period of harsh dismissal of them in the face of globalized market relationships' (Schuller, Baron and Field, 2000, 13).

At the same time, in the UK new social policies were and are increasingly directed towards building individual and community capacity in order to encourage individual and social responsibility for well-being, for example through health education or in the work of children's centres or community schools. What we are seeing, therefore, is a move away from simply delivering services. Particularly prominent in recent times (though far from new) has been the concentration on 'parenting deficits', weak social ties and the social ills arising from these. Such social problems have prompted interventions designed to build individual capacity and responsibility, through parental education and family centres for example.

The continuing problem of social inequalities in participation, new directions in social policy[4] and the concomitant disillusion with lifelong learning policies have led to a renewed interest in the social outcomes of learning in the policy and academic communities. A focus on the links between improved health outcomes, length of education and level of education has been particularly prominent. This relationship is a complex one and data are often difficult to interpret.[5] For example, does good health mean that an individual is likely to take greater advantage of educational opportunities or does more education somehow lead to better health? Alternatively, is it in fact socio-economic status which matters here, conferring better health on those in higher socio-economic groups *and* ensuring that they have higher educational qualifications as well? There is strong evidence to suggest that participation in education can lead to health benefits such as the adoption of healthy behaviours and in supporting individuals through life transitions (Hammond, 2002). However, as Hammond notes, there are a range of factors to be taken into account that present a complicated pattern of relations and the magnitude of any correlation depends on what is being measured – for example life expectancy or the incidence of depression. One important point highlighted by Hammond is the operation of the inverse care law, which means that those in higher socio-economic groups and most likely to be healthy are also most likely to access and use health services (especially secondary healthcare services in hospitals) most successfully. This may lead to underestimations of the incidence of morbidity in some socio-economic groups. What emerges here is a pattern of some complexity and breadth, which represents a search for 'new' ways of explaining the continued exclusion of particular social groups. Prominent amongst these is a concern with the potential social benefits of learning to families, individuals and communities and a renewed interest in the idea of social capital.

Social capital and the social benefits of learning

In Chapter 2, we discussed Bourdieu's concept of cultural capital and the way in which Bourdieu understood the three types of capital he identifies (economic, social and cultural) as interlinked (Bourdieu, 1997). He defined social capital as the resources arising from engaging in a durable network or networks that are characterised by reciprocity and mutuality. This might be relatively institutionalised, as in membership of a political party or a professional association; or relatively informal, such as membership of a babysitting exchange or an extended family. Central to Bourdieu's analysis is that all forms of capital are unequally distributed across the population. Bourdieu was trying to explain the reproduction of privilege in schooling and he developed his theory as a way of explaining the different ways in which working-class children might face processes of exclusion in school. The significance of his contribution is that it provides a theoretical framework for identifying and explaining the social processes involved in social disadvantage and as a result his work has been highly influential. For Bourdieu then, people with high levels of social capital are likely to be those with high levels of other sorts of capital. Here we explore the development of the concept of social capital which has been particularly influential in contemporary research and theory in education and is increasingly influential in policy making.[6]

It is perhaps not surprising that social capital has been of particular interest in adult education which has always had a strong tradition of interest in and working with communities. The contemporary focus on 'community schools' in various forms, community-based and 'owned' services and 'joined-up' government also creates conditions in which the concern with *social connections, healthy communities* and *social cohesion* has moved to centre stage. In this way the idea of social capital resonates with current social policy discourses about 'what matters'. However, approaches vary considerably in the way that social capital is understood, its significance and methods of measuring it. While some writers in the area of education have drawn on Bourdieu's approach, most notably Ball (2003, 2006) in his exploration of the way in which middle-class parents use social capital at their disposal to obtain places at 'desirable' schools for their children, other researchers and writers have looked elsewhere. Particularly prominent and often cited is the work of Coleman (1988) and Putnam (2000).[7] Coleman examined educational attainment in American communities and was interested in the ways in which social relationships served as a useful resource for families and communities. His work was primarily focused on families and he identified various aspects of families (such as family form) that might generate social capital. Coleman believed that two-parent families would have greater levels of social capital than one-parent families, for example. Social capital in Coleman's work is not something that is deliberately deployed to gain advantage – as in Ball's (2003) analysis – but something that is acquired as a result of participation in activities almost as a by-product (Croll, 2004). Morrow (1999) has criticised Coleman for portraying women's employment negatively and for his support for the patriarchal family, which is portrayed as possessing higher levels of social capital. Unsurprisingly, perhaps, the role of children in generating social capital inside and outside families is not considered by Coleman.[8] While Coleman focused on the family and its networks, Putnam (2000) looked beyond the family in his study of political and civic participation. In his widely cited book *Bowling Alone*, he argued that social capital in America was in decline as demonstrated by decreased levels of participation in sports and leisure activities. Putnam and Coleman depart from Bourdieu in that they regard social capital as a fairly accessible resource. For both writers, social capital is not entirely determined by other sorts of capital and neither is it (necessarily) used or obtained by individuals or groups at the expense of others. In a discussion of Coleman and Putnam's conceptions of social capital, Croll (2004) notes that '. . . social capital is . . . an entirely non-zero sum and non-competitive commodity. Far from one person's social capital being at the expense of others, it actually enhances that of others'. (pp. 400–401)

This extremely compelling 'benign' view of social capital is characterised by a number of features, which tend to present social capital as an accessible resource, as non-competitive, as linked to values of trust and reciprocity and traditional notions of the family combined with concerns about the *decline* in contemporary civic society and family life. These various features of the 'benign' view of social capital resonate with an expansive range of political and social concerns. While Coleman and Putnam's work could be considered to be politically conservative, the commitment to a vital civic society is also attractive to the political centre and the political left. The idea that social capital is not the preserve of the privileged has proved attractive to theorists and practitioners who have emphasised the social and cultural strengths of working-class communities (see Crowther, 2004 and Martin, 2003, for example.) The concern with the potential decline of civic society, trust and reciprocity has attracted a number of researchers who have sought to test these assumptions by measuring the strength of social capital using a number of indices. Li, Savage and Pickles (2003), for example, use the British Household Panel Survey data from 1992 to 1999 in order to examine membership of groups and hence civil engagement over time, and in particular, differences in engagement by social class. A number of findings indicate clear differences between social classes along with some gender differences. Individuals who had been upwardly mobile were less likely to be engaged in civic organisations than others in their destination class indicating that their class origin continued to be of relevance. Women were less likely to be civically engaged and poorly educated women were shown to be the least likely to be a member of any civic organisation. This is particularly significant given that people who are *not* civically engaged are less likely to participate in adult learning. Similarly, in a study of the incidence of informal learning, Gorard, Fevre and Rees (1999) also found gender differences and noted that women's informal learning activities were more likely to generate social capital than were men's. Li, Savage and Pickles' findings present a complicated picture of class differences and fluidity in types of memberships of civic organisations. They relate this partly to changes in class identities but do not find evidence for a *general* decline in social capital though they identify falling levels of social capital for the working class.

Similarly, Grenier and Wright (2003) argue that there are widespread and growing differences across the population in participation in community organisations. Thus, they found that members of the middle and upper classes were twice as likely to belong to at least one community organisation as unskilled manual workers. They found that fewer people were volunteering but that those that did gave more time. Perhaps, crucially, given the current governmental focus on young people, the young and the unemployed volunteer less. However, this trend may not be a result of declining levels of reciprocity and mutuality so much as the professionalisation of the voluntary sector. Grenier and Wright also point out that we do not have enough data on the informal networks used by women and that consequently we may actually be underestimating levels of social capital in communities. Interestingly, they note a trend towards participation in activities and groups where there are low levels of personal interaction. Again Gorard, Fevre and Rees's (1999) study of informal learning provides *some* support for this position, noting a decline in interest in local history and politics but a rise in keeping pets, using a computer[9] and sports activities. Grenier and Wright's main conclusion is that growing inequality in society is of central importance when considering social capital, since rising inequality is likely to result in declining levels of trust:

> . . . class based divisions which constrain participation remain deeply embedded and result in significant drag to efforts to increase and broaden social capital. The distribution of participation is not a niggling concern – it is the main story, with important implications for social trust as well . . . concerns about inequality, social class, and workplace protections, may actually be critical to effective strategies to support the development of social capital.
>
> (2003, 24)

In summary, the differences in Coleman and Putnam's approaches and Bourdieu's highlight the contentious issue of whether or not social capital operates exclusively and therefore whether or not it is a private or a public good. In other words, to what extent is social capital deployed competitively to achieve positional and private advantage as opposed to simply operating benignly to confer advantage generally to communities and individuals? Of relevance here is evidence on class differences in social and civic participation. However, these are not easily measured.

Linking social capital and learning

The nature and operation of social capital is of increasing interest in the adult education literature most notably in the work of Field (1999, 2005), Schuller, Baron and Field (2000) and Schuller *et al.* (2004). Schuller, Baron and Field (2000) describe social capital as, '. . . social networks, the reciprocities that arise from them, and the value of these for achieving mutual goals'. (p. 1). In a later publication, Field (2005) describes the core elements as personal connections, interpersonal interaction and shared values. Crucially, here social capital is not the prerogative of the privileged: Field describes social capital as '. . . a distributed resource, which is not the exclusive property of the privileged elite, but is also created and mobilised by subordinate and intermediary groups of all kinds' (2005, 28). However, he does acknowledge that social capital may be used to maintain privilege and that there are important social class differences to consider. For Field, these class differences are also cross-cut by other social distinctions, such as lifestyle, so that differences in the accumulation of social capital across social groups are not reducible to class differences alone.

Field identifies a number of ways in which social capital may be linked with participation in learning. First, social capital may be seen as a network supplying resources which will influence access to information, skills and knowledge about opportunities. Second, networks in themselves are learning resources supplying useful informal and formal information depending on the nature of the network. Third, there is considerable evidence that individuals who are civically engaged are more likely to participate in learning. The relationship between social capital and learning is not uncomplicated, however. This is partly because it is two-way, with high educational attainment likely to lead to high levels of social capital, while high levels of social capital are likely to facilitate higher levels of educational attainment. Field's analysis relies on extensive research in Northern Ireland – a society characterised by strong traditional networks and high educational attainment in young people, especially when compared with the much more limited involvement of adults in learning. Field argues that the nature of social capital generated by traditional networks which are localised and relatively segregated in working-class communities is supportive of schools and that this is an important contributing factor in explaining high achievement in young people. However, it appears to be less supportive of adult participation.

The research found varying attitudes towards learning amongst adults, which Field explains partly by pointing out that people have access to different types of social capital. He explains these qualitative and quantitative differences in social capital by drawing on Woolcock's (Field, 2005) typology of social connection and describes three categories of social connection with implications for lifelong learning:

- Bonding social capital
- Bridging social capital
- Linking or scaling social capital.

In the first of the three categories, social ties are highly localised, although there is limited access to information outside of local networks. This is likely to mean traditional support for schools. Bridging social capital describes social ties which, although they may be less localised, exist between similar types of people, bringing increased opportunity for knowledge exchange. Accordingly, individuals' relationships with the education system are highly context-specific. Finally, linking social capital includes dispersed ties with 'unlike' individuals and means greater opportunity for knowledge exchange and individual change.

Therefore it is not merely the size but the nature of the social networks that matters. This is likely to differ depending on social position. Some networks may be more useful than others for 'getting on in life' and Croll (2004) reminds us that this is encapsulated in the phrase 'to be well connected'. Again, it is important to point out at this juncture that the issue of adult participation in learning and its links with social capital are complex. First, there is no simple division between participation and non-participation and the importance of informal learning cannot be underestimated, though it is often relatively invisible. Second, networks are not simply important for the ways in which they contribute to knowledge transfer but also for the wide range of resources which they offer. Field highlights, for example, the affective aspects of social capital and the kinds of social literacies that they may generate. Thus, '. . . people who acquire their social literacy from their bonding ties will find that they lack critical capabilities – including affective ones such as confidence – when they move beyond the borders of their existing community of practice.' (2005, 150). There is some overlap here with Schuller's (2004) concept of identity capital discussed in Chapter 2. One potential (though not inevitable) danger here, as we noted in Chapter 2, is that there will be a focus on the deficits of excluded groups while ignoring the strategies of exclusion operated by particular social groups (Preston, 2004). For Preston, these strategies of exclusion raise the important issue of distribution of resources, inequality and social justice.

It is evident that there are a number of tensions in the various theories informed by concepts of social capital with differing emphases being placed on the definition and the operation of social capital by different intellectual camps (Li, Savage and Pickles, 2003). This has led to considerable differences of emphasis being placed on key elements. The main tensions are between the following: social capital as private positioning or public good; the extent to which it fosters connectedness or creates divisions; the extent to which theorists emphasise the deadening effect of growing inequality or the agency of working-class communities in generating useful social capital and finally the extent to which economic relations are emphasised or not. There is thus considerable criticism of and debate around the differing assumptions underlying the concept, its theoretical 'pedigree' and the way in which it has been deployed and operationalised in research.

Problems with social capital theory

Fine (2001) offers a comprehensive critique of the way in which the concept of social capital is understood and deployed. First, he argues that the link between social and economic capital and the reproduction of privilege is largely ignored and that reference is most often made instead to the politically conservative formulations of Putnam and Coleman. For Fine, the conceptual divisions made between social and economic capital are artificial because all capital is social in nature and simply moves through different forms. He argues that this glossing over of the significance of economic relations means that social capital theories have been attractive across the political spectrum to the left and the right. For example, it is possible that social capital approaches could be deployed in policy to argue for support for traditional family forms or to argue for community development policies aimed at social and political empowerment of excluded communities (see Chapter 8 on community learning). Underplaying the link between the economic and the social leaves economic inequality unchallenged and civic society may then be focused on in isolation from economic relations and the state:

> capital is only appropriately understood as social from the outset in the economic relations that it encompasses. Any use of the term social capital . . . is an implicit acceptance of the stance of mainstream economics in which capital is first and foremost a set of asocial endowments possessed by individuals rather than, for example, an exploitative relation between classes and the broader social relations that sustain them.
>
> (Fine, 2001, 38)

What Fine is arguing here is that social networks are inextricably enmeshed in economic relations. He believes that the tendency to leave capitalist-economic relations unchallenged found in classical economics is now colonising social science more generally and that this has a number of negative consequences. First, it may mean that a deficiency of social capital may be seen purely as an individual failure as '. . . something that the unsuccessful lack . . .' (2001, 108) and that this simply legitimates economic inequalities. Second, it underplays the potential for social capital to be deployed in ways that are exclusionary, for example the use of networks to capture positional goods to the detriment of others, such as a place in a 'good' school or an 'elite' university. Third, Fine argues that it is undermining theory production which, in the case of 'social capital theories', are overly general, universalistic and ahistorical. Capital in all its forms, he argues, is highly socially specific, changing from place to place and over time – and yet there is a failure to specify the concept of social capital in any but the most general terms. This inevitably leads to problems of measurement and an over-reliance on metaphors or proxy variables such as health outcomes as a means of measuring levels of social capital in a given community. This, in turn, makes the leap from social capital theories to policy recommendations problematic, so that '. . . the idea of building social capital as a development policy borders on the nonsensical . . . statements about what it is and what effects it has are either vacuous or non generalisable from specific instances'. (p. 199)

Fine's critique is helpful in that it highlights the dangers of ignoring the interplay between different forms of capital which he so clearly identifies. It also reminds us of the consequences of social capital's so called 'dark side' – the entrenchment of privilege. He may also be right about trends in social theory production, although Field (2005) notes that the current interest in social capital may just as easily represent the societalisation of economic theory. Field also contends that there is nothing in Bourdieu which would undermine the view that social capital may be connected, yet at the same time may also be relatively autonomous from economic capital and that it is not therefore exclusively the preserve of the privileged. Arguably, there is nothing intrinsic to the concept itself that makes it universalistic, though it has undoubtedly been used in this way and it is possible to envisage further specification of social capital which might give it greater social specificity. Measuring social capital with a view to achieving policy recommendations is highly problematic but this is a general problem in social science.[10] Finally, some of Fine's criticisms are also found in Blaxter and Hughes' (2000) critique of the concept when they characterise it as '. . . an economic model with a community face' (p. 90). They also argue that the literature on social capital is largely gender blind, ignoring the issue of how social capital is *created* in communities and families and by whom. They are also concerned that parental deficit theories (and the very real policy interventions that are generated by them) are part of a disciplinary discourse directed at women who are 'failing' to fulfil traditional roles. As Blaxter and Hughes note,

> whenever the term parent is invoked the speaker really means mothers . . . when we discuss the poor we should note that the majority of the world's poor are women. . . . When we argue for the bonds of collectivities to be strengthened who do we think is already doing the bulk of this unpaid emotional and physical work?

> (2000, 87)

Social purpose, critique and utility

The renewed concern with the social benefits of learning, and with social capital and the critique of lifelong learning policies and practices as overly economistic, raises the following question of social purpose: What are we trying to achieve in adult learning? This has usually been regarded as a highly political question in adult education and it has been a central focus in the 'social purpose tradition'. Indeed, some writers have called for a return to the traditional concerns of 'social purpose' in critiques of lifelong learning discourses (see Crowther, 2004; Kane, 2007; Martin, 2003; Shaw and Martin, 2000; Steele, 2000, for example). Others have drawn on this tradition in critiques of some contemporary postmodern engagements with lifelong learning policies and practices (Taylor, Barr and Steele, 2002). In a discussion of popular education in Latin America and elsewhere, Kane (2007) has argued that lifelong learning provision and practices are sites of struggle around the issues of purpose and social justice potentially opening up spaces for broader debates and alternative practices within mainstream provision despite their seeming 'economism'. The recent broadening of the debate as represented in the renewed interest in the social dimensions of lifelong learning may be just such an example of this kind of struggle. Here, we briefly consider the relevance of the social purpose tradition and its relationship to the contemporary focus on the issue of social capital and the social benefits of learning. The point here is to widen the parameters of the debate and to further emphasise the historical specificity of these different formulations of the social dimensions of adult education and learning.

The social purpose tradition belongs to adult education discourses and practices rather than contemporary lifelong learning discourses, and has its roots in nineteenth- and twentieth-century social and economic relations. We define it rather generally and inclusively here. It incorporates a cluster of related values but diverse practices, which are highly specific to particular contexts. This includes elements of liberal and radical traditions of thought which have their roots in particular political contexts. In the case of the radical tradition, this includes a concern with social inequality and social justice, a concern with power relations and their relationship to knowledge and importantly, a critique of mainstream education. Globally, practices are incredibly diverse including democratic or community-focused education[11] as well as revolutionary practices such as popular education in Latin America,[12] informal learning and political activities within social movements in Western democracies[13] and the university extension movement of the nineteenth-century Britain – a forerunner of university adult education.[14] In other words, the social purpose tradition has expressed itself in a great variety of ways that are highly dependent on the political and social context. In the British context, key issues include a concern with the relationship between knowledge and power; a focus on movements for social change and a critique of the relationship between the state and education.

In a seminal article *Really Useful Knowledge: Radical Education and Working-class Culture, 1790–1848*, Richard Johnson (1979) discusses the origins of modern adult education in the radical social movements of the nineteenth century. The article itself grew out of a resurgence of the political left in Western Europe in the 1960s and 1970s. Following the disillusionment with Communism in the former Soviet Union, there emerged in Britain (and elsewhere in Europe) an intellectual and political movement known as the 'New Left' which revisited Marxist theory in an attempt to broaden its relevance by shifting away from the narrow economistic concerns with class and production to one which took account of gender, race relations and the importance of culture and consumption. The work of the Centre for Contemporary Cultural Studies at the University of Birmingham, where Johnson was working when he wrote this piece, made an important contribution to this intellectual and political ferment[15] which was intellectually connected to popular, community and university adult education. A central concept often referred to in writings is that of 'really useful knowledge'. The idea of 'really useful knowledge' was an outgrowth of popular social movements in the nineteenth century which sought to resist mainstream education and training which they saw simply as narrow and utilitarian – 'merely' useful knowledge. 'Really useful knowledge' by contrast was conceptualised as broader and socially critical incorporating a radical and political education, as democratising and ultimately emancipating. A cardinal element of this tradition is its *oppositional* nature and its rejection of the utilitarian. Johnson's account links this tradition with nineteenth-century popular social movements and the influence of a flourishing radical press.

In the twentieth century similar links were made between the social purpose tradition and social movements such as the women's movement as well as in community politics, often played out in state-funded community development and community education (Coats, 1994; Mayo, 1997; Thompson, 1997). Such social movements and community action provided critiques of social inequality in twentieth-century Britain and critiques of mainstream education. This some-times resulted in far-reaching changes to curricula, particularly as a result of feminist critiques which, for example, raised awareness of sexism in children's literature and reading schemes as well as providing scholarly critiques of the ways in which women's social and historical contributions had been overlooked in academic disciplines. Finally, Johnson argued that radical adult education has certain key features: its oppositional nature, the development of alternative goals and the development of a varied educational practice. The contemporary sig-nificance of the 'social purpose' tradition and its historical legacy is disputed. While some see this tradition as comprising the core values of adult education practice, others maintain that this was essentially a minority tradition. These differences are expressed in both theory and practice. We do not pursue that debate here.

The relevance of this discussion is that the *contrasts* between social capital theory and the social purpose tradition alert us to the historically specific ways in which the social dimensions of adult education are expressed in educational the-ory and practices. In the contemporary concern with the social benefits of learning and in the development of social capital theories, we find a response to and, in some cases, a critique of the economism of lifelong learning. We also find, to some extent, a focus on individual agency within networks. Governmental agendas in emphasising the social benefits of learning are ambiguous and have been criticised as utilitarian or obscuring issues of poverty and growing inequality – '. . . an eco-nomic model with a community face' (Blaxter and Hughes, 2000, 90). Some of these issues are taken up in the critiques of social capital theory. At the same time, there are *similarities* between social purpose and social capital accounts. In partic-ular, both are, at least potentially, oppositional in character and have the capacity to generate alternative educational goals and practices. In that sense there are clear affinities between them, so that contemporary 'social capital approaches' may be seen as a palimpsest of the social purpose tradition. It remains to be seen whether or not the critiques of social capital approaches are justified or whether social capital approaches have the capacity to further widen the debate beyond issues of economy and competition, to generate new theories and practices and to address the extremely entrenched problem of educational inequality in the learning society.

Notes

1 A useful summary of this thematic review is available from the Learning and Skills Development Agency in Policy Briefing Paper 30 (LSDA, 2003).

2 These are Canada, Denmark, Finland, Norway, Portugal, Spain, Sweden, Switzerland and the UK (in fact it includes England only).

3 See St Clair (2006) for a useful review of survey evidence on the persistence of class inequalities in adult participation.

4 As Field (2006) points out, this represents a significant shift in the relationship between individuals and the state and one that is evident in lifelong learning policies as well as in social policies.

5 See Groot and van den Brink (2007) for a technical discussion of these difficulties.

6 See, for example, Scottish Executive (2004).

7 See Schuller, Baron and Field (2000), for a useful summary and Croll (2004) and Morrow (1999) for useful critiques.

8 The agency of children is in fact rarely considered rendering their participation and contribution to social networks invisible. However, see McGonigal et al. (2007) who give this some consideration.

9 One problem here is that of changing definitions of social interaction in the networked society. The question is whether participation in MySpace, Internet dating, Youtube, Freecycle, ebay and the like generates significant social capital or not and moreover whether any social capital thus generated may be considered a public or a private good.

10 See Cavaye (2005) and Field and Osborne (2006) for discussions of issues of measurement in assessing social capital.

11 See Lovett (1988) on the 'radical' tradition in adult education, Martin (1996) on community education in the twentieth century and Lovett (1975) on class and community development. Thompson (1995) includes a range of critical essays on changes in adult education which start from a radical approach. Fieldhouse (1996) offers a comprehensive history of adult education in Britain in the nineteenth and twentieth centuries.

12 The seminal text here is Friere (1996) (revised edition). See Kane (2007) for a contemporary analysis.

13 Johnson (1979) gives an account of the relationship between the 'social purpose' tradition and nineteenth-century popular movements. Note that an abridged version of Johnson's article is available in Thorpe, M., Edwards, R. and Hanson, A. (1993). Crowther, Martin and Shaw (eds) (1999) offer a range of essays exploring the links between social movements and popular education in Scotland. Colley, Hodkinson and Malcolm (2003) offer a useful overview of different types of informal learning including popular education.

14 The university extension movement of the late nineteenth century began with the provision of lectures outside Oxford and Cambridge, which were made available to individuals who would not at that time have been admitted to Oxbridge (middle-class women, for example). It failed to reach significant numbers of working-class students who could not afford the fees. Nevertheless, it represents an early move to democratise access to education for adults and is an antecedent of the Workers Educational Association established in 1903. In the early years of the twentieth century, Oxford established a network of extramural activities and this extramural tradition was established in other universities following the Great War and which gained ground as the century wore on giving rise to an adult and continuing education tradition with which significant twentieth-century academics were engaged.

15 Important writers here include (for example) E.P. Thompson (Thompson, 1994) and Raymond Williams (see McIlroy and Westwood, 1993). Also useful for a flavour of these issues and times are Wainwright (1994, 2003), Ali (1987) and Hall (1988).

References

Ali, T. (1987) *Street Fighting Years: An Autobiography of the Sixties.* London: Collins.

Ball, S. (2003) *Class Strategies and the Education Market: The Middle Classes and Social Advantage.* London: RoutledgeFalmer.

Ball, S. (2006) *Education Policy and Social Class: The Selected Works of Stephen J Ball.* London: RoutledgeFalmer.

Blaxter, L. and Hughes, C. (2000) Social capital: A critique. In Thompson, J. (ed.) *Stretching the Academy: The Politics and Practice of Widening Participation in Higher Education.* Leicester: NIACE.

Bourdieu, P. (1997) The forms of capital. In Halsey, A. *et al.* (eds) *Education Culture Economy Society.* Oxford: Oxford University Press.

Cavaye, J. (2005) Social capital: A commentary on issues, understanding and measurement. In Duke, C., Osborne, M. and Wilson, B. (eds) *Rebalancing the Social and the Economic: Learning Partnership and Place.* Leicester: NIACE.

St Clair, R. (2006) *Looking to Learn: Investigating the Motivations to Learn and the Barriers Faced by Adults Wishing to Undertake Part-Time Study.* Edinburgh: Scottish Executive, http://www.scotland.gov.uk/Publications/2006/03/09075850/0 (accessed 20 May 2007).

Coats, M. (1994) *Women's Education.* Buckingham: Society for Research in Higher Education and Open University Press.

Coleman, J. S. (1988) Social capital in the creation of human capital. *American Journal of Sociology* 94: 95–120.

Colley, H., Hodkinson, P. and Malcolm, J. (2003) *Informality and Formality in Learning: A Report for the Learning and Skills Research Centre.* London: Learning and Skills Development Agency.

Croll, P. (2004) Families, social capital and educational outcomes. *British Journal of Educational Studies* 52(4): 390–416

Crowther, J. (2004) 'In and Against' lifelong learning: Flexibility and the Corrosion of Character. *International Journal of Lifelong Education* 23(2): 125–136.

Crowther, J., Martin, I. and Shaw, M. (1999) *Popular Education and Social Movements in Scotland Today.* Leicester: NIACE.

Field, J. (1999) Schooling, networks and the labour market: Explaining participation in Northern Ireland. *British Educational Research Journal* 25(4): 501–516.

Field, J. (2005) *Social Capital and Lifelong Learning.* Bristol: Policy Press.

Field, J. (2006) *Lifelong Learning and the New Educational Order.* Stoke on Trent: Trentham Books.

Field, J. and Osborne, M. (2006) Researching social capital in Europe: Towards a toolkit for measurement. In Duke, C., Doyle, L. and Wilson, B. (eds) *Making Knowledge Work: Sustaining Learning Communities and Regions.* Leicester: NIACE.

Fieldhouse, R. (ed.) (1996) *A History of Modern British Adult Education.* Leicester: NIACE.

Fine, B. (2001) *Social Capital Versus Social Theory: Political Economy and Social Science at the Turn of the Millennium.* London: Routledge.

Friere, P. (1996) *Pedagogy of the Oppressed*. Harmondsworth: Penguin.

Gorard, S., Fevre, R. and Rees, G. (1999) The apparent decline of informal learning. *Oxford Review of Education* 25(4): 437–454.

Grenier, P. and Wright, K. (2003) *Social Capital in Britain: An Update and Critique of Hall's Analysis*. London: Centre for Civil Society, London School of Economics, http://www.lse.ac.uk/collections/ccs/publications/iwp> (accessed 4 May 2007).

Groot, W. and van den Brink, H. (2007) The health effects of education. *Economics of Education Review* 26: 186–200.

Hall, S. (1988) *The Harsh Road to Renewal: Thatcherism and the Crisis of the New Left*. London: Verso (in association with *Marxism Today*).

Hammond, C. (2002) What is it about education that makes us healthy? Exploring the education-health connection. *International Journal of Lifelong Education* 21(6): 551–571.

Johnson, R. (1979) 'Really useful knowledge': A radical education and working class culture, 1790–1848. In Clarke, J., Critcher, C. and Johnson, R. (eds) *Working Class Culture: Studies in History and Theory*. London: Hutchinson.

Kane, L. (2007) Conflict and cooperation between 'popular' and 'state' education in Latin America. *Journal of Adult and Continuing Education* 13(1): 53-67.

La Valle, I. and Finch, S. (1999) *Pathways in Adult Learning Research Report RR137*. Norwich: Department for Education and Employment.

Learning and Skills Development Agency (LSDA) (2003) *Policy Briefing Paper 30 Beyond Rhetoric: Adult Learning Policies and Practices OECD Review of Adult Learning*. London: LSDA, http://www.lsda.org.uk/policy/BriefingPapers.aspx (accessed March 2007).

Li, Y., Savage, M. and Pickles, A. (2003) Social capital and social exclusion in England and Wales (1972–1999). *British Journal of Sociology* 54(4): 497–526.

Lovett, T. (1975) *Adult Education, Community Development and the Working Class*. London: Ward Lock Education.

Lovett, T. (ed.) (1988) *Radical Approaches to Adult Education*. London: Routledge.

Martin, I. (1996) Community education: The dialectics of development. In Fieldhouse, R. (ed.) *A History of Modern British Adult Education*. Leicester: NIACE.

Martin, I. (2003) Adult Education, lifelong learning and citizenship: Some ifs and buts. *International Journal of Lifelong Education* 22(6): 566–579.

Mayo, M. (1997) *Imagining Tomorrow: Adult Education for Transformation*. Leicester: NIACE.

McGonigal J., Doherty R., Allan, J. *et al.* (2007) Social capital, social inclusion and changing school contexts: A Scottish perspective. *British Journal of Educational Studies* 55(1): 77–94

McIlroy, J. and Westwood, S. (1993) *Border Country: Raymond Williams in Adult Education*. Leicester: NIACE.

Morrow, V. (1999) Conceptualising social capital in relation to the well-being of children and young people: A critical review. *The Sociological Review* 47(4): 744–765.

Organisation for Economic Co-operation and Development (OECD) (2003) *Beyond Rhetoric: Adult Learning Policies and Practices*. Paris: OECD.

Preston, J. (2004) Lifelong learning and civic participation: Inclusion, exclusion and community. In Schuller *et al.* (eds) *The Benefits of Learning: The Impact of Education on Health, Family Life and Social Capital*. London: Routledge.

Putnam, R.D. (2000) *Bowling Alone: The Collapse and Revival of American Community*. New York: Simon and Schuster.

Schuller, T., Baron, S. and Field, J. (2000) Social capital: A review and critique. In Baron, S., Field, J. and Schuller, T. (eds) *Social Capital Critical Perspectives.* Oxford: Oxford University Press.

Schuller, T., Hammond, C., Basset-Grundy, A., Preston, J. and Bynner, J. (2004) *The Benefits of Learning: The Impact of Education on Health, Family Life and Social Capital.* London: Routledge.

Scottish Executive (2004) *Working and Learning Together to Build Stronger Communities: Scottish Executive Guidance for Community Learning and Development.* Edinburgh: HMSO.

Shaw, M. and Martin, I. (2000) Community work, citizenship and democracy: Remaking the connections. *Community Development Journal* 35(4): 401–413

Steele, T. (2000) Common goods: Beyond the new work ethic to the universe of the imagination. In Thompson, J. (ed.) *Stretching the Academy: The Politics and Practice of Widening Participation in Higher Education.* Leicester: NIACE.

Taylor, R., Barr, J. and Steele, T. (2002) *For a Radical Higher Education: After Postmodernism.* Buckingham: The Society for Research into Higher Education and the Open University Press.

Thompson, E. P. (1994) *Making History: Writings on History and Culture.* New York: The New Press.

Thompson, J. (1995) *Adult Learning: Critical Intelligence and Social Change.* Leicester: NIACE.

Thompson, J. (1997) *Words in Edgeways: Radical Learning for Social Change.* Leicester: NIACE.

Thorpe, M., Edwards, R. and Hanson, A. (1993) *Culture and Processes of Adult Learning.* London: Routledge.

Wainwright, H. (1994) *Arguments for a New Left: Answering the Free-market Right.* Oxford: Blackwell.

Wainwright, H. (2003) *Reclaim the State: Experiments in Popular Democracy.* London: Verso.

Chapter 4

The economics of lifelong learning

'Middle aged workers whose skills become obsolete make poor investments. The young and the more able make good investments' (Heckman and Masterov, 2005, 107–108). These are the words of a Nobel Prize winning economist that present a challenge in discussing the economics of investing in later life. However, despite the possible discomfort of such a statement, it is undeniable that if rates of return on investment in human capital were the sole reason for taking part in learning, there are instances where this would not be a rational economic choice. The social and economic imperatives for lifelong learning are often debated in ways that oppose the two. However, in practice they are intertwined. Even within an area such as widening participation to higher education with its emphasis on equity of opportunity, there are strong economic imperatives at the level of individuals, universities and government. At all of these levels, widening participation is viewed as a means not only of social inclusion, but one which will both improve the economic prospects of individuals and of the nation as a whole. For Higher Education Institutions (HEIs), quasi-markets and increasing competition for students within an expanded Higher Education (HE) system have meant that new student markets have had to be found to sustain economic viability. These 'new' markets include, in part, those who have traditionally been socially excluded. This chapter explores both the perceived and real economic benefits to individuals, organisations and national economies in investing in lifelong learning.

Lifelong learning and economic imperatives

When lifelong education first became a subject for debate in the 1970s with the publication of the Faure Report for UNESCO *Learning to Be* (1972), the conceptual and rhetorical basis of the issues being discussed was clearly all-encompassing.

> Every individual must be in a position to keep learning throughout his life. The idea of lifelong education is the keystone of the learning society. The lifelong concept covers all aspects of education, embracing everything in it,

with the whole being more than the sum of its parts. There is no such thing as a separate "permanent" part of education which is not lifelong. In other words, lifelong education is not an educational system but the principle in which the over-all organization of a system is founded, and which accordingly underlies the development of each of its component parts.

1972, 181–182

The successor UNESCO report *Learning: The Treasure Within* (UNESCO Commission on Education, 1996), stresses the link between lifelong learning and social stability. Nevertheless, in many countries around the world the strategic direction of lifelong learning policy in recent times has focused primarily on economic outcomes and therefore on those of working age. Medel-Añonuevo, Ohsako and Mauch (2001, p. 4) summarise this changing emphasis over the last few decades in arguing that,

lifelong education in the early 1970s was associated with the more comprehensive and integrated goal of developing more humane individuals and communities in the face of rapid social change. On the other hand, the more dominant interpretation of lifelong learning in the nineties was linked to retraining and learning new skills that would enable individuals to cope with the demands of the rapidly changing workplace.

Reports from international and trans-national bodies such as *Lifelong learning for All* (OECD 1996, 1999) and the *Memorandum on Lifelong Learning* (EC, 2001), although always acknowledging the social, emphasise the economic rationale for lifelong learning. For example, within Europe it is possible to observe a succession of policy statements which argue that the education and training systems of the countries of the European Union must show adaptability to the new demands of the knowledge society and meet the challenge of improving the level and quality of employment. It is argued that learning opportunities need to be centred around the requirements of particular target groups at different stages of their life course. Learning therefore should not be directed towards young people only, but also, in particular, towards unemployed adults and those in employment whose skills are not sufficient to adapt to rapid industrial and technological change.

Frequently quoted is the Lisbon Strategy of the Council of the European Union (2000, para 5) (the forum for the Union's political leaders), which set the objective of making the European Union the 'most dynamic and competitive knowledge-based economy in the world, capable of sustainable economic growth with more and better jobs and greater social cohesion' by 2010. This objective was crystallised in 14 quantitative targets related to objectives concerned with economic growth, employment, social inclusion, education, region development and environmental matters. Subsequent policy statement assert the link between lifelong learning and achieving the economic, employment and social goals for Europe set out in the Lisbon strategy. Since then, a range of measures have been put in place that seek to support member states in the implementation of the strategies for achieving the agreed goals. In these strategies, there is an emphasis on the role of Vocational Education and Training (VET) (i.e. provision directly linked to the development of human capital and employment), in parallel with general and higher education. A subsequent Council of the European Union (2003) highlighted 'using benchmarks to identify best practice and to ensure efficient and effective investment in human resources'. One of these benchmarks is that the EU average level of participation in lifelong learning should be at least 12.5 per cent of the adult working age population (the 25 to 64 age group) (EC 2004, 14). This and other benchmarks are also used as indicators to monitor Guideline 23 of the employment policies of the Member States of the EU, namely to 'Expand and improve investment in human capital'.[1]

These EU policies and accompanying rhetoric present a model of education and learning as principally one of economic investment in human capital. The human capital arguments found within the European Union are echoed elsewhere with high profile management theorists such as Drucker (1999) and political economists such as Reich (1991) arguing for the need for skilled 'knowledge workers' in the 'new economy' of the twenty-first century. Watson (2003) in her review of lifelong learning policy in Australia provides a cogent overview of the work of these writers, and shows how much of this thinking has penetrated national level policy debates in her own country. She quotes, for example, a report commissioned by State and Territory Ministers of Vocational Education and Training that prioritises the need to invest in 'Australian skills and innovative capacities' as follows: 'Competing in the knowledge economy is primarily competition in building intangible capital, and particularly human capital – essentially skills and knowledge and the ability to carry those into work processes and to adapt and innovate' (Fitzgerald 2001, 1).

Similar sentiments are found in the US, where a report for the Federal government states that 'Americans in the 21st Century workplace will need to continuously upgrade their skills and knowledge as new technologies and work patterns emerge' (U.S. 21st Century Workforce Commission, 2000, 57).

In particular, this and other reports emphasise the changes in working life that are a function of modern information and communication technologies (ICTs). Such issues also surface in the developing economies, including that of China, for example.

Modern distance education is a new type of education that has come into being with the development of modern information technology. It is a major means to build up a lifelong learning system meeting the needs of people living in an era of knowledge economy.

(Ministry of Education, 1998, para 20)

Certainly, skills deficits are seen as a challenge in many economies in the world. Many countries perceive that a lack of adequately trained workers threatens national competitiveness in global markets, and the UK provides a good example of the complex factors in action when the economic aspects of lifelong learning provision are considered. Recent analysis of the skills base of the UK reveals considerable challenges that are manifested in some stark data and comparisons. Seven million adults lack functional numeracy and five million lack functional literacy and amongst the 30 countries of the OECD, the UK ranks 18th for low skills and 11th for high skills. Thirty-five per cent of working age population do not have a full Level 2 National Vocational Qualification (NVQ) and 36 per cent are qualified to intermediate level (Level 2–3 in the NVQ framework), compared with over 50 per cent in comparable countries such as Germany and New Zealand. Such data have been highlighted by the Leitch Review of Skills (HM Treasury, 2006), which points out a number of economic and social challenges faced both at a national and international level, and by government, businesses and individuals. The argument of this report is that the skills of the UK are not world-class and that there is a risk that this will undermine the country's long-term prosperity. Further, because the UK's productivity continues to trail many of its main international comparatives, and much more needs to be done to reduce social disparities, Leitch argues that 'improving our skill levels can address all of these problems.'(p. 1) In other words, it is argued that improving skills addresses issues of competitiveness and the continuing problem of social exclsuion.

Such improvements are not simply about improving *initial* education and training in this nation's economy. A recent Learning and Skills Council report (LSC, 2006) argues that *continuing* VET to upgrade and reskill will be an urgent requirement for two main reasons. First, the report argues that in most occupational areas required skill levels will increase and many current skills will no longer be relevant. Second, for reasons of demography there will be a declining number of young people entering the workforce from 2010 and this means a greater reliance on the current workforce. This may mean that England will also have to look beyond the current working population and its existing school population for skills. One implication, therefore, is that migrants may be key to meeting skills needs, and this will have particular implications for the nature of lifelong learning. A further implication of trends in the UK is that greater efforts may have to be directed towards reskilling those currently within the benefit system so that they can be moved into work. The aim to reduce welfare expenditure, where possible, is an important element in maintaining national competitiveness. Placing greater responsibilities on individuals, encouraging them to take responsibility for their employability by reskilling is one aspect of this strategy. As we argue in other chapters, this represents a change in the relationship between individuals and the state. However, the economic costs in moving the most socially excluded into employment may be considerable.

Economics for individual learners

At an individual level it is the benefits associated with employability, whether this entails obtaining a job or career promotion, that are seen as prime motivators for participation in post-compulsory education and training. And there certainly is much evidence, particularly amongst adults, that economic motives associated with professional and career advancement are important motivators for considering an engagement in lifelong learning. For example, in a major study of the decision-making processes of adults considering a return to higher education, almost all individuals interviewed were motivated by the thought of a 'better job' (Davies and Williams, 2001). 'Better' meant, especially for single parents, a passport to a secure and well-paid future. Others, often those already established in a career, wanted an advanced qualification in order to make progress in their chosen fields. Of course, economic considerations were not the only motivations. Other individuals were looking for future employment that they would find interesting and stimulating rather than simply financially rewarding. These factors linked to personal advancement are found in a number of other similar studies (e.g. Woodley and Brennan, 2000 and Woodley, 2001). At the same time, prospective students are often acutely aware of the economic costs and potential risks of participation. The risks associated with taking the plunge into higher education counterbalance the perceived benefits for students described by Davies and Williams (2001) for example. Amongst the factors perceived to be impediments to their study and related work (see Osborne, Gallacher and Crossan, 2004) are cost of studying; the need to work to earn a living; responsibilities of current job; domestic/family responsibilities; lack of childcare; lack of confidence; the system of state benefits; and fear of long-term debt. The majority of these factors are economic and lie at one level within the domain that Cross (1991) described as 'situational', namely the result of life circumstances. They also relate to the lack of quality of information upon which to base rational economic decisions and attitudinal factors including aversion to debt. This mix of social and economic factors underline the complexity of motivation and decision-making. 'Rational' economic decision models are therefore of limited use in understanding decision-making.

Clearly, the anticipation of long-term benefit of any sort is difficult to disentangle from current costs. For example, Osborne, Gallacher and Crossan (2004) found that respondents who were single parents were adamant about the need for additional help if they were to be able to square the circle of studying and caring for a family given their existing personal economic circumstances. These caring relations are highly gendered, as we note in Chapter 2 and this highlights both the complexity of social and economic factors involved and the influence of socio-economic status on decision-making.

There is a considerable literature that assesses the economic return from investing in education leading to qualifications with wage[2] normally being used as the measure of benefit. In the UK, for example, studies by the Centre for the

Economics of Education (Dearden *et al.*, 2000 and McIntosh, 2004) have computed such benefits and provide a comprehensive overview of the complexity of doing so. The detail in such analyses provides a complex picture, but benefits certainly depend on type of qualification achieved. For example, it is reported by McIntosh (2004, 31) that individuals who did not acquire any qualifications while at school, can receive positive returns from achieving a wide range of qualifications in post-compulsory schooling, in particular, vocational qualifications. However, these qualifications provide no further benefits to individuals who had already achieved five or more good General Certificate of Secondary Education (GCSEs) or 'A' levels at school. Indeed, he also provides evidence that for those who achieve this level of school performance the only awards that provide an economic benefit are degrees and professional qualifications with, in the case of women only, the caveat that some other HE qualifications provide a return. The analysis also indicates that average relative returns from having a HE qualification have not changed over time, and this is despite the significant expansion of the UK system in the period under study (1993–2002). It is estimated that the average difference in earnings during this time period for someone holding an undergraduate degree is 24–29 per cent higher by comparison with someone who does not, controlling for all other certificated educational attainments. Indeed Chevalier and Walker (2001) show that, in spite of the massive expansion of the system, the average private return for graduates in the UK has remained constant for the preceding two decades as demand for graduate level skills has increased. Demand for graduate skills appears to have increased in line with an increase in the availability of graduates. It is worth pointing out here that this may reflect credential inflation as much as anything else. In other words, the increase in graduates may mean that employers are able to recruit graduates to positions that previously did not require graduate qualifications. This underlines the fact that ideas about 'skills' are socially as well as economically constructed thus adding further complexity to arguments about 'reskilling'.

Whilst there is considerable evidence of there being an economic benefit from achieving qualifications there are many caveats. Again using the UK as a case, affordability and benefit have been major issues since the introduction of tuition fees with HE in England. In an expanding HE system with considerable institutional differentiation in terms of prestige, selectivity in choosing students and funding, a key question is whether there are differential outcomes in attending different types of HEIs. In the US there has been much research in the area and, for example, it is reported by Brewer, Eide and Ehrenberg (1999) that the more expensive and prestigious private institutions provide significantly higher financial returns than their lower costing public counterparts. There is less research of this kind in the UK, not least of all because of the absence of a significant non-publicly subsidised sector. But with the decline of such subsidy over time, and the most elite institutions arguing for differentially higher fees on the basis of providing commensurate benefit, Chevalier and Conlon have investigated this proposition. They suggest that there is an 'increase in earnings derived by graduates from prestigious universities' which ' stems from an increase in human capital rather than signalling or network effect, as it appears to be constant over time' (2003, 19).

One consequence of such findings is that there indeed might be an argument for differential fees, and that a common fee at all institutions means a greater subsidy to those attending the most prestigious HEIs. It also raises issues in relation to widening participation in the UK, and the fact that there is still, despite the policies to create greater opportunity for traditionally non-participating groups, especially those with lower social economic status, differentiation by type of HEI attended. Indeed it might be argued that certain forms of widening access, such as the encouragement of links between Further Education Colleges (FECs) and HEIs sustain this inequity since these arrangements largely direct adults and those from lower socio-economic groups to less prestigious universities and potentially poorer labour market outcomes (Osborne and MacClaurin, 2006).

Costs and benefits for older learners

When we consider the economic benefits of learning in later life, the picture is more complex. A number of economists have calculated the economic rate of return on human capital at different stages of the life cycle. For a given monetary investment, there is a diminishing return over time, since the earlier the investment the greater the time horizon over which returns can be made. Similarly, such models would argue that optimal human capital investment is not only made towards the young, but also to the already most skilled and most literate (see Heckman, 2000 and Carniero and Heckman, 2003). The argument here is that 'early investments raise the productivity (lower the costs) of later investments' (Heckman and Masterov, 2005, 48) and that there is a synergistic effect. 'Learning begets learning; skills (both cognitive and non-cognitive) acquired early on facilitate later learning' (p. 48).

Egerton (2000, 289) has pointed out that several factors have been found to lower the pay of mature graduates including, socio-economic status, type of HEI attended, location where employment is most likely to be secured and sector of employment. And although for most individuals there is a private economic benefit from participation as adults that benefit is difficult to compute (Conlon, 2002), though delaying the investment in education is likely to reduce that benefit. For example, Wolter and Weber (1999) show that in Switzerland if at age 40 a male invests in either an academic or vocational degree, he would reduce the present value of his lifetime earnings. Two clear issues for adults in any computation of returns are costs while studying and forgone income. If an individual enters any form of education at the expense of employment then not only it is likely that costs are incurred, but also the opportunity to earn and to receive and make contribution to future benefits is diminished. For example, it is likely that for many employer contributions to a pension at retirement would be lost. When these calculations are fed into the wage equation, then a different picture emerges. Furthermore, decisions upon which qualification to undertake might be based not only on those that offer the highest annual return, but also on cost and duration. So, for example, in the UK despite the lower return on a short cycle qualification such as a Higher National Certificate/Diploma by comparison to a degree (see McIntosh, 2004 for details), their duration of one or two years if taken on a full-time basis might be a sensible decision for adults at certain points in their life.

We must also take into account the costs of study. Taking again the UK HE as a case, although it has high levels of student retention by OECD standards at around 80 per cent, there is considerable variation by institution, and with the widening of participation there have been anxieties that this proportion will decrease. A recent report by the National Audit Office (2002) has shown that mature students are more likely to drop out than those under 21 at entry. A report on student retention (Universities UK, 2001) had already highlighted a number of problems that are experienced by undergraduate students. Of these factors and perhaps the most crucial are the increased financial constraints associated with study: as a consequence more students are now working during term-time than ever before, and the anti-social nature of some of these working hours is having deleterious effects upon their studies (see Barke *et al.*, 2000; Brennan *et al.*, 1999; Independent Committee of Enquiry into Student Finance 1999; Kember, 1999;Brennan *et al.*, 1999). Perceptions of debt certainly have been, and remain, critical to mature students' decisions to enter (and remain) in HE in the UK. This is particularly true for those from poorer backgrounds (CVCP, 1998). Callender and Kempson (2000) found that students from higher socio-economic groups receive the most in terms of parental contributions and gifts. Mature students have the highest levels of spending on *essential* items, not least of which is childcare needs (Davies, Osborne and Williams, 2002 and Osborne *et al.*, 2001) and are most likely to take out student loans to meet essential needs. This is certainly suggestive of a financial divide between rich traditional age students and (relatively) poor mature students.

One clear area of differentiation in relation to benefit is the relative return for those already in work and those who are unemployed. Jenkins (2004) in a longitudinal study of women in the UK has established a strong association between 'adult learning and the probability that women who were out of work in 1991 returned to work between 1991 and 2000, even after controlling for a range of family and economic circumstances which also influenced employment transitions'. The learning in adulthood here was defined in terms of acquiring a qualification from the age 33 to 42. In an earlier study using similar data Jenkins *et al.* (2003) had reported that adult learning leading to a qualification seemed to have little or no impact on earnings. It is therefore argued that 'this evidence on the economic effects of lifelong learning supports the view that such learning is more effective in enhancing the employment prospects of those out of work than in improving rewards for those already in work' (Jenkins, 2004, 21).

Benefits to society

Economic benefit is not simply restricted to gains made by individuals. Arguments relating to competitiveness focus not only on the individual, but also companies[3] and national economies as a whole. Furthermore, there may be indirect economic benefits at a societal level, and these might justify a range of interventions by governments on the grounds of efficiency of use of resources. However, the OECD reports that 'gains to society at large over and above those received by individual investors in lifelong learning' might justify interventions, perhaps in the form of subsidies by government, but the 'existence of such externalities is often asserted rather than supported by empirical evidence' (OECD, 2001, 46). One area where there is clear evidence of societal benefit exists and concomitantly justification for government intervention is in fact based on US studies of investment in early childhood education and care. This investment according to human capital models not only leads to private returns, but is linked to wider economic benefits as measured by a reduction in the unit costs of primary and secondary schooling, greater completion rates and subsequent reductions in receipt of welfare, teenage pregnancy and crime (Verry, 1998). The outcomes of a number of interventions of this type are summarised by Heckman and Masterov (2005, 76–84). These authors in a later work also provide arguments for investing in disadvantaged children, arguing both for individual and societal gain:

> We argue that, on productivity grounds, it makes sense to invest in young children from disadvantaged environments. Substantial evidence shows that these children are more likely to commit crime, have out-of-wedlock births and drop out of school. Early interventions that partially remediate the effects of adverse environments can reverse some of the harm of disadvantage and have a high economic return. They benefit not only the children themselves, but also their children, as well as society at large.
>
> (Heckman and Masterov, 2007, 2).

Otherwise economic arguments that might justify government action are largely linked to job-related general training where subsidies have been offered to encourage companies to make such provision. *General Training* refers to a situation where 'a trainee's productivity is increased wherever the trainee is employed subsequently' and is contrasted with *Specific Training* that 'only increases the productivity in the firm providing the training' (OECD, 2001, 47). The necessity of subsidy relates to the anticipation by firms that generally trained employees will be lost to other companies, and without it there would be a sub-optimal amounting of training.

Concluding remarks

Even if investing in lifelong learning in later life produces less tangible economic benefits to society at large it is still of course merited because of the strong association between private economic benefits and level of qualification at most points within the life course, subject to certain caveats. The evidence of benefit exists, though, as we have indicated, the type of qualification taken, mode of study, opportunity cost and the point at life at which engagement with learning takes places are all important factors in computation of benefit. In pure economic terms, it may yield no benefit at all as Heckman and Masterov (2005) have argued for middle-aged workers. Better they argue to subsidise the employment of displaced older workers.

Certainly the consideration of rates of return on investment in education and training is a factor that influences policy formation. However, such an approach is fraught with difficulties since such methods have largely been applied within the formal sector, and are concerned with certificated qualifications. It is notable that in our account in this chapter, we have not concerned ourselves with the economics of non-certificated informal and non-formal lifelong learning, which are more difficult to measure. As the OECD (2001,145) points out in the context of lifelong learning 'rate of return and other forms of programme evaluation are plagued by the non-availability of data, the heterogeneous nature of provision, the often informal nature of provision (as in many types of in-service training), the small scale of some demonstration programmes, etc'. It is therefore evident that benefits beyond the economic necessarily have and will play a key role in policy debate.

It is also important to note, as we signalled in our introduction, that paralleling the economic agenda are social concerns and these are not mutually exclusive. It is common in many arguments concerning economic benefit to also focus on issues such as social inclusion and equity, and there has been particular focus on the unequal distribution of opportunity to those from lower socio-economic group and particular ethnic minority backgrounds in many debates internationally. That being said, a number of policies, which in their rhetoric make links between the social and the economic, may in practice stress the economic – an accusation that has been levelled by some critics at the Lisbon Agenda. Perhaps it is the Leitch Review in the UK (HM Treasury, 2006, p. 9), which most neatly sums up some of the linkages stating,

> Skills are a key driver of fairness; unequal access to skills has contributed to relatively high rates of child poverty and income inequality in the UK. There are clear links between skills and wider social outcomes, such as health, crime and social cohesion.

We might also consider that in a world of rapid technological change some past investments in human capital can become suddenly obsolete. This certainly implies that upgrading of knowledge and skills is required throughout an individual's working life to maintain the value of human capital. And whilst Heckman and Masterov (2005, 2007) have argued that the returns of late investment to those with lower prior educational investment are low, the returns of late investment to those who have had past investment, which is now obsolete, may be higher because of the capacities created by the earlier investment. A further argument might be that there are major societal and economic benefits in keeping older individuals who so choose in work, a pre-requisite for which may be continuing learning. Not only might such people contribute directly through their productivity and the taxes that they pay, but also their dependency on the state is reduced since they would not be receiving benefits. Furthermore, there is some evidence that continuing learning in later life has health benefits (Aldridge and Lavender, 1999) and it is conceivable that such engagement in itself reduces costs to the state.

Perhaps, arguments relating to economic benefit whether to individuals or nations may have to be adjusted in the future as the demography of many nations changes. Whilst early investment creates greatest benefit, if populations of young people are declining more rapidly than demand for skills increases, investments in the older may increase returns relative to the past. As our financial advisers say, past returns are not reliable indicators when making investment for the future.

Finally, there are important points to be made about inequalities between social groups in achieving a good rate of return on investments made. Average rates of return hide inequalities between the most and least prestigious institutions in higher education, for example. Inevitably, parental support in young undergraduates is stronger in higher socio-economic groups potentially reducing the individual costs to those students. Credential inflation may have reduced the positional advantage of having a university degree. Keep and Mayhew (2004) suggest that whilst numbers of graduates increase, numbers of 'better jobs' do not increase at the same pace. Moreover, accessing the highest paying jobs is not simply a matter of human capital but also of social and cultural capital and these are unevenly distributed. Not all of those who even achieve access to the most prestigious institutions can compete equally for these jobs, since their stock of social capital will be used in further shifting (see Brown, 2003). Finally, the increase in the number of graduates exacerbates relative disadvantage for those who do not achieve graduate status.

Notes

1 For those interested in the full range of EU policies in relation to Education and Training, we recommend using the EC (2007), which provides access to all main documentation since the Lisbon Council of 2000. The extent to which the Lisbon Goals at its mid-term are on target to be achieved is discussed by Morgensen, Lenian

and Royuela-Mora (2004). Amongst other issues raised by these authors are the inadequacy of data, and it might be added that the measure of lifelong learning, namely an involvement in learning during the previous four weeks by the relevant age cohort at an appointed census point, has considerable limitations in itself for policy making. Critics such as the European Trade Union Confederation (ETUC) (2006) have argued that in its first phase the Lisbon Agenda has 'an excessive emphasis on labour market flexibility and competition, and neglect of the social dimension'. European Commission President José Manuel Barroso relaunched the Lisbon Strategy in 2005 as a *Partnership for Growth and Jobs* (EC, 2005) with simplified targets and reporting procedures for member states. See http://ec.europa.eu/ireland/general_information/key_issues/growth_and_jobs/index_en.htm for more information on the Lisbon agenda.

2 Wolf (2004) points out economists use simple proxies. Levels of earnings are equated to individuals' marginal product, that is, their bit of contribution to gross domestic product. Those with more education earn more and the argument follows that they contribute more to productivity. She points out, however, that first the higher earnings of individuals are not simply a function of their education, but are also related to other personal abilities they possess and that second, using the proxy of higher wages to represent higher productivity is not as strong as economists suggest.

3 We discuss this further in Chapter 7.

References

Aldridge, F. and Lavender, P. (1999) *Impact of Learning on Health*. Leicester: NIACE.

Barke, M., Braidford, P., Houston, M., Hunt, A., Lincoln, L., Morphet, C., Stone, I. and Walker, A. (2000) *Students in the Labour Market: Nature, Extent and Implications of Term-time Employment Among University of Northumbria Undergraduates*. DfEE Research Report 215. London: HMSO.

Brennan, J., Mills, J., Shah, T. and Woodley, A. (1999) *Part Time Students and Employment: Report of a Survey of Students, Graduates and Diplomates*. London: Centre for Higher Education Research and Information/Department for Education and Employment.

Brewer, D., Eide, E. and Ehrenberg, R. (1999) Does it pay to attend an elite private college? *Journal of Human Resources* 33: 104–123.

Brown, P. (2003) The opportunity trap: Education and employment in a global economy. *European Educational Research Journal* 2(1): 142–180.

Callender, C. and Kempson, M. (2000) *Changing Student Finances: Income, Expenditure and the Take-up of Student Loans Among Full- and Part-time Higher Education Students 1998/9*. DfEE, Research Report 213. London: HMSO.

Carneiro, P. and Heckman, J. (2003). Human capital policy. In Heckman, J. and Krueger, A. (eds) *Inequality in America: What Role for Human Capital Policy?* Cambridge, MA: MIT Press.

Chevalier, A and Conlon, G. (2003) *Does it Pay to Attend a Prestigious University?* London: Centre for the Economics of Education.

Chevalier, A. and Walker, I. (2001) Returns to education in the UK. In Harmon, C., Walker, I. and Westergaard-Nielsen, N. (eds) *Education and Earnings in Europe*. Cheltenham: Edward Elgar.

Committee of Vice-Chancellors and Principals (CVCP) (1998) *From Elitism to Inclusion: Good Practice in Widening Access to Higher Education*. London: CVCP.

Conlon, G. (2002) One in three? The incidence and outcomes associated with the late attainment of qualifications in the United Kingdom. *Journal of Adult and Continuing Education* 8(1): 14–45.

Council of the European Union (2000) *Lisbon European Council Presidency Conclusions*. 23 and 24 March 2000, at http://www.europarl.europa.eu/summits/lis1en.htm

Council of the European Union (2003) *Council Conclusions on Reference Levels of European Average Performance in Education and Training (Benchmarks)*, at http://ec.europa.eu/education/policies/2010/doc/after-council-meeting_en.pdf

Cross P. (1991). *Adults as Learners*, 2nd Edition. San Francisco: Jossey Bass.

Davies, P. and Williams J. (2001). For me or not for me? Fragility and risk in mature students' decision making. *Higher Education Quarterly* 55(2): 185–203.

Davies, P., Osborne, M. and Williams, J. (2002) *For Me or Not for Me? That is the Question: A Study of Mature Students' Decision-making and Higher Education*. DfEE, Research Report No. 297. England: DfEE, at http://www.dfee.gov.uk/research/query.cfm?cat=2

Dearden, L., McIntosh, S., Myck, M. and Vignoles, A. (2000) *The Returns to Academic, Vocational and Basic Skills in Britain*. Skills Task Force Research Paper 20.

Drucker, P.F. (1999). Knowledge-worker productivity: The biggest challenge. *California Management Review* 79 Winter.

Egerton, M. (2000). Pay differentials between early and mature graduate men: The role of state employment. *Journal of Education and Work* 13(3): 289–306.

European Commission (2001) *The Memorandum on Lifelong Learning*, at http://www.bologna-berlin2003.de/pdf/MemorandumEng.pdf

European Commission (2004) *Progress towards the Common Objectives in Education and Training – Indicators and Benchmarks*, at http://ec.europa.eu/education/policies/2010/doc/progress_towards_common_objectives_en.pdf

European Commission (2005) *Working together for Growth and Jobs: A New Start for the Lisbon Strategy*, at http://ec.europa.eu/growthandjobs/pdf/COM2005_024_en.pdf

European Commission (2007) *'Education & Training 2010' – Main Policy Initiatives and Outputs in Education and Training Since the Year 2000*, at http://ec.europa.eu/education/policies/2010/doc/compendium05_en.pdf

European Trade Union Confederation (ETUC) (2006) *The European Union's Lisbon Strategy*, at http://www.etuc.org/a/652

Faure, E. (1972). *Learning to Be: The World of Education Today and Tomorrow*. Paris: UNESCO.

Fitzgerald, V. (2001) *Skills in the Knowledge Economy: Australia's National Investment in Vocational Education and Training*. Canberra: The Allen Consulting Group.

Heckman, J. (2000) Policies to foster human capital. *Research in Economics* 54(1): 3–56.

Heckman, J.J. and Masterov, D.V. (2005) *Skill Policies for Scotland*. The Allander Series, Glasgow: University of Strathclyde, at http://www.fraser.strath.ac.uk/Allander/Allander%20Papers/Heckman.pdf

Heckman, J.J. and Masterov, D.V. (2007) *The Productivity Argument for Investing in Young Children*. Bonn: Forschungsinstitut zur Zukunft der Arbeit.

HM Treasury (2006) *Prosperity for all in the Global Economy – World Class Skills, The Leitch Report*. London: HMSO.

Independent Committee of Enquiry into Student Finance (1999) *Student Finance: Fairness for the Future*. Edinburgh: Independent Committee of Inquiry into Student Finance.

Jenkins, A. (2004) *Women, Lifelong Learning and Employment*. London: Centre for the Economics of Education.

Jenkins, A., Vignoles, A., Wolf, A. and Galindo-Rueda, F. (2003) The determinants and labour market effects of lifelong learning. *Applied Economics* 35: 1711–1721.

Keep, E. and Mayhew, K. (2004) The economic and distributional effects of current policies on higher education. *Oxford Review of Economic Policy* 20(2): 298–314.

Kember, D. (1999) Integrating part-time study with family, work and social obligations. *Studies in Higher Education* 24(1): 109–124.

Learning and Skills Council (LSC) (2006) *Skills in England 2005*, Vols 1–3. London: LSC.

McIntosh, S. (2004) *Further Analysis of the Returns to Academic and Vocational Qualifications*. London: Centre for the Economics of Education.

Medel-Añonuevo, C. Ohsako, T. and Mauch, W. (2001) *Revisiting Lifelong Learning for the 21st Century*. Hamburg: UIE, at http://www.unesco.org/education/uie/publications/uiestud28.shtml

Ministry of Education (1998) *Action Scheme for Invigorating Education towards the 21st Century – People's Republic of China*, at http://www.ilo.org/public/english/employment/skills/hrdr/init/chn_3.htm#Modern

Morgensen, U.B., Lenain, P. and Royuela-Mora, V. (2004) *The Lisbon Strategy at Mid-Term; Expectations and Reality*. Warsaw: Center for Social and Economic Research.

Organisation for Economic and Co-operation and Development (OECD) (1996) *Lifelong Learning for All*. Meeting of the Education Committee at Ministerial Level, 16–17 January 1996. Paris: OECD.

Organisation for Economic and Co-operation and Development (OECD) (1999) *Science, Technology and Industry Scoreboard 1999 Benchmarking Knowledge-based Economies*. Paris: OECD.

Organisation for Economic Co-operation and Development (OECD) (2001) *Economics and Finance of Lifelong Learning*. Paris: OECD.

Osborne, M. and MacClaurin, I. (2006) A probability matching approach to FE/HE transition. *Journal of Higher Education* 52(1): 149–183.

Osborne, M., Gallacher, J., and Crossan, B. (eds) (2004) *Researching Widening Access*. London: Routledge.

Osborne, M. *et al.* (2001) *For Me or Not for Me in Scotland? A Report of Mature Student Participation in Higher Education*. Report Prepared for the Scottish Executive. Glasgow and Stirling: Centre for Research in Lifelong Learning.

Reich, R. (1991) *The Work of Nations: Preparing Ourselves for 21st Century Capitalism*. New York: Alfred A Knopf.

UNESCO Commission on Education (1996). *Learning: The Treasure Within*. Report to UNESCO of the International Commission on Education for the Twenty-first Century. Paris: UNESCO.

U.S. 21st Century Workforce Commission (2000) *A Nation of Opportunity: Building America's 21st Century Workforce*, at http://digitalcommons.ilr.cornell.edu/key workplace/21

Verry, D. (1998) *Some Aspects of Early Childhood Education and Care*. Discussion Paper 98-06. London: University College London, Department of Economics.

Watson, L. (2003) *Lifelong Learning in Australia*. Canberra: DEST.

Wolf, A. (2004) Education and economic performance: Simplistic theories and their policy consequences. *Oxford Review of Economic Policy* 20(2): 315–333.

Woodley, A. (2001) Learning and earning: Measuring 'rates of return' among mature graduates from part-time distance courses. *Higher Education Quarterly* 55(1): 28–41.

Woodley, A. and Brennan, J. (2000) Higher education and graduate employment in the United Kingdom. *European Journal of Higher Education* 35(2): 239–249.

Wolter, S.C. and Weber, B.A. (1999) Skilling the unskilled – A question of incentives? *International Journal of Manpower*, 20(3–4): 254–269.

Chapter 5

Lifelong learning and schools

The 'problem' of schooling

Until recently, schooling was largely ignored in the adult education literature except where it was identified, usually in passing, as part of the problem. Schools were criticised as conservative, isolated institutions that were teacher rather than learner focused. It was argued that education was too 'front-ended' in that policy and resources were over-committed to initial education. The consequences of this are an inadequate emphasis on learning later in life with all the social and economic benefits that this could deliver. In addition to these criticisms, schools have long been condemned for helping to reproduce and even to reinforce socio-economic inequalities of opportunity.[1] For many (perhaps optimistic) adult education practitioners, participation in adult education offered an antidote to the 'problem' of mainstream provision, offering a second chance to those who had been failed by the school system and in some cases an alternative curriculum and teaching practice designed to challenge mainstream practices and characterised as 'alternative' or 'radical'. These criticisms predate the current focus on lifelong learning.[2]

In the contemporary context, there are clearly some problems with a position, which essentially ignores schooling. First, schools are constantly changing. Despite the sense we may have of them as monolithic, unchangeable institutions, in historical terms, mass schooling is a relatively recent development and schooling has changed considerably in a fairly short time. For example, schools are now (arguably) more learner focused, and more connected to communities and to the rest of the education system than in the past. These developments highlight issues such as community participation, increasing capacity in communities and building learner motivation and are therefore highly relevant to participation in education later in life. Moreover, research has consistently shown that initial success in education makes participation in both formal and informal education and training later in life much more likely. Even if one disagrees with current visions of the learning society promoted by national governments, the crucial role of schooling in ensuring participation later in life cannot be ignored.

Contemporary moves towards a learning society both in policy and in practice bring us to a second strand of criticism of schools and provide the main focus for our discussion in this chapter. This strand is in fact a cluster of concerns expressed mainly by policy makers, national governments and supra-national organisations, most notably the OECD. The concern is that schools *must* change in order to play their part in the creation of a learning society. In the UK, particularly in England, this includes a complex range of related agendas. First, there is a concern with *efficiency* and the idea that schools should be 'effective' and accountable along particular dimensions and thus deliver competitive outcomes. This is often expressed as 'raising standards'. Second, schools are also subject to the perceived need for *public sector reform* in general and in particular, reform of working practices, decision-making and – to some extent – in funding. Third, in England, there is a threefold push towards greater *diversity* in provision, for *personalised learning* and finally for greater *integration* of schools into the wider education system as well as into local communities. Therefore, the relationship between school reform and the creation of a learning society in practice is not a simple one. Unsurprisingly, it is influenced by changing political fashions as well as the changing role of the state in society. New policies are always controversial. Some fear that the integration of schooling into the lifelong learning agenda will make schooling too instrumental, for example. So the idea that the school curriculum should reflect the changing needs of the 'knowledge economy' is contentious. Similarly, greater parental choice and diversity of provision raise pressing questions about the inclusion of vulnerable groups in areas where there is competition for school places. This chapter will unravel some of this complexity in order to examine the implications of lifelong learning for schools. We begin with a discussion of the concerns expressed by the OECD in recent publications before proceeding to consider the relationship between schools and lifelong learning under four headings: *competence and competition*, the *learner-centred school*, the *connected school* and *schooling in the future*.

Do schools need to change?

In its *Schooling for Tomorrow* series (OECD, 2001) and elsewhere (OECD, 2005a, 2006), the OECD considers the extraordinary changes confronting schools including the contemporary emphasis on children's rights and voice, changing social attitudes to schools (e.g. less deference on the part of pupils and parents) and the changing media engagements of school pupils who are some-times referred to as the 'digital generation'. Moreover, schools are confronted with an increasingly diverse range of pupils, cultures and curricula while society itself is characterised by greater diversity of family form and types of employ-ment. At the same time, inequality persists in educational attainment across social groups in OECD countries[3] with significant proportions of pupils failing to achieve. Finally, of course, lifelong learning discourses insist on the *necessity* of change in the face of the advent of the 'knowledge economy' and the consequent increase in global competition. For this reason it is argued that schools should abandon standardised, inflexible practices sometimes referred to as 'the factory model' in order to engage all pupils and become learning organisations.

> Lifelong learning means... ensuring that schooling prepares young people well for a life of learning.... Education systems need to pay greater attention to improving broad cognitive and motivational outcomes of schooling. ... schools will have to transform, ensuring that their staff are themselves lifelong learners, and that they become innovative as organisations...
>
> (OECD, 2005a, 76)

The OECD (2005a) identifies four features of lifelong learning that have implications for schools. First, the idea that all organised learning should be interconnected, thus facilitating learning over the lifespan and learning pathways through different types of learning and qualifications as appropriate. This is already important in post-compulsory education and training. This will affect schools by fostering a variety of links between schools and other educational institutions. An example of this connectivity common to a number of countries is the creation of national qualification frameworks (NQFs) which facilitate educational pathways and student transfer between institutions and levels via agreed, transparent definitions of awards and credits (Young, 2003). Freer movement of older school pupils between Further Education Colleges (FECs) and schools in the UK is another example of greater connectivity and greater permeability of institutional boundaries. The main implication here is that schools are not detached or isolated from the rest of the education system. Second, lifelong learners should be at the centre of the learning process. In England this is often expressed as the need for personalised or tailored learning, which is discussed below. Third, education should be concerned with student motivation and engaging all learners. Finally, education is presented as having multiple objectives. It is not just about meeting economic imperatives (OECD, 2005a), something that the lifelong learning agenda has been persistently criticised for.

Thus the OECD (2005a) proposes a five-dimensional framework for pursuing lifelong learning in schooling systems:

- Professional development of teachers
- Learner-centred schools
- Multiple objectives of education
- Focus on the motivation to learn
- Systemic and inter-connected schools.

These will of course be realised (if at all) in different ways by different countries. Before considering these issues further, there is one more issue of concern that deserves mention. The OECD (2005a) among others (Instance, 2003 and Schuller *et al.*, 2004) have questioned the sustainability and desirability of continually extending the period of initial education. This trend is a consequence of the tendency of national governments to set targets for increasing participation in upper secondary and tertiary education. It could be argued that this makes education too front-ended and does not, in fact, necessarily encourage participation throughout the life cycle. Moreover it creates relative disadvantage for those who do *not* stay on. In addition, there is the question of the economic sustainability of extending the period that young people remain in education. Young people have been entering the workforce at an increasingly late age, so that across the OECD, up until the age of 30 the average 15-year-old can expect to spend as much time in education as in work (6.4 years) (OECD, 2006). At the same time the population of many OECD countries is ageing. By mid-2025, in England and Wales, for example, the proportion of the population of pensionable age is projected to increase to 24 per cent (Gask, 2006, 9). This raises three questions. First, at what point do high proportions of economically inactive individuals in the population become economically unviable? Second, how can the education system meet this challenge? Instance (2003) discusses the possibility of lowering the school-leaving age and creating opportunities to move in and out of education later on. In England, it is notable that proposals to make participation in some form of education and training for 16–18-year-olds, with sanctions for those who do not comply, take policy in a very different direction (DfES, 2007).[4] Other solutions may be to accelerate learning cycles, a course of action which would obviously be highly controversial in the case of children. Lastly, what are the social consequences of extended adolescence such as higher numbers of young people in their twenties living in the parental home, particularly given the upward trend in separation and divorce of the parent generation? Therefore, quite apart from the educational issues posed by reforming schooling, wider social change serves both to effect *and* to result from changes in schools.

In summary, the OECD voice a number of concerns about how well schools are contributing to lifelong learning and they suggest a number of areas of focus for policy and practice. While they are sensitive to the criticism of being too economistic, this does not mean that they are not concerned (some may argue pre-occupied) with the *utility* of schools or school outcomes and it is this issue to which we now turn.

Competence and competition

Increased economic competition between countries does not just focus attention on the quality of the labour force; it also places restraints on public expenditure and, arguably, on what individual governments can achieve in policy and practice. This places pressure on the public sector, including the education system, which is expected to maintain or improve achievements often with limited resources. This demands stringent economy and efficiency. Increasingly, governments expect 'value for money' and this has meant concentrating on specified outcomes, measuring individual and institutional performance and, finally, target-setting as a means of ensuring that schools are 'effective'. In England, there has been a great deal of change in schooling over the last twenty years. This has resulted in demanding school inspection regimes, greater control of the curriculum from the centre and the production of school league tables – to name a few examples. These developments have been hotly contested (see Ball, 1998, 2006; Slee, Weiner and Tomlinson, 1998). Nevertheless, league tables and other performance measures are often reported in the popular media in ways that have emphasised school failure. Common themes of this discourse of failure are falling standards; 'dumbing down' – such as exams that are supposedly too easy – and poor pupil performance in key skills such as reading and maths. It hardly needs saying that this is a challenging environment for schools and policy makers alike.

In addition to these issues of competitiveness and effectiveness, there is a related concern with the competence of individual pupils and the changing competencies necessary for a changing economy. The argument here is that the 'knowledge economy' demands new kinds of skills (most obviously information technology skills) and new dispositions, such as the need for individual flexibility, initiative and responsibility in a rapidly changing labour market. Individuals and economies without these skills will, it is argued, be left behind. This raises some issues and challenges. First, there is a concern that such a focus might mean that school curricula become narrow, utilitarian and centrally controlled by government. Indeed, some would contend that this is already the case. Yet this development is by no means inevitable and it partly depends on how and what key competencies are defined as important. Perhaps the most developed attempt to define in addition to measuring relevant competencies is found in the Programme for International Student Assessment (PISA), which was launched by the OECD in 1997. This began with an assessment of student performance of 15-year-olds in maths, reading, science and problem-solving in each of the 30 OECD countries. This has produced a wealth of data that compares performance between and within countries. Three findings are relevant to this discussion of competence and lifelong learning: the first of these is the finding that significant proportions of students in OECD countries fail to achieve basic levels of competency. For example, mathematical literacy[5] is measured along a number of dimensions on a scale of 1-6 with level one being the most basic level. All OECD countries with the exception of two have at least 10 per cent of students who perform at only level 1 or below.[6] It is worth noting in general here that there are significant disparities in performance between countries – with the potential for these to grow. This is clearly an issue of competitiveness for some countries. A range of findings on reading literacy also support the finding that significant proportions of populations fail to achieve basic or benchmark levels (OECD, 2006). Second, student socio-economic status continues to influence achievement.

Across countries, students from the least socio-economically advantaged backgrounds are on average 3.5 times more likely to be low mathematics performers, i.e. at or below level 1, than those from the most socio-economically advantaged backgrounds.

(OECD, 2006, 83)

Moreover, the data indicate that schools may actually reinforce these inequalities. We should note here that these data are a starting point only, since making meaningful international comparisons is problematic. For example, age groups will be at different stages in their schooling from country to country and cultural differences may also affect the ways in which tests are taken by students in different countries (Brown, 1998). Finally, there has been a significant extension of education expectancy.[7] This rose by an average of 1.5 years between 1995 and 2004 in OECD countries (OECD, 2006).

What are we to conclude from these findings, which represent just fragments of the international data now regularly gathered by the OECD? The increase in education expectancy looks like good news for lifelong learning. However, the tendency for governments to set targets for higher participation in upper secondary and tertiary education as a way of creating a learning society is, as we have already noted, criticised by some (Instance, 2003) on the grounds that it exacerbates the 'problem' of front-ended systems by extending the *initial* period of participation in education. Moreover, an increase in education expectancy does not necessarily mean a decrease in educational inequality because it tells us nothing about *who* is enjoying the longest education expectancy. The disparities in student attainment and proportion failing to achieve at basic or benchmark levels would seem to be bad news. The reasons for such 'failure' are less easy to assess. Indeed some (Slee and Weiner, 1998) have criticised the undue emphasis on attainment as too narrow, arguing instead for greater attention to be payed to context and culture and stressing the need to avoid approaches which are too concerned with economy and efficiency. For Slee and Weiner, research which has focused on school effectiveness in this way has obscured important issues such as inequality, social inclusion and pupil identity. In the UK context, some writers have maintained that research data purporting to assess school effectiveness quantitatively have instead been used to monitor and manage schools in ways that have shifted control away from education professionals in educationally and politically undesirable ways (Ball, 2006; Lingard, Ladwig and Luke, 1998; Kelly, 1999). The argument here is that there is a discourse of effective schooling that is reductionist, in that it focuses on some quantitative outcomes, neglecting other issues and that these are driven by economic and technocratic aims. Ultimately, it is important to remain critical of analyses that fail to acknowledge that there is disagreement about what constitutes 'effectiveness'. Nevertheless, this does not invalidate the relevance of the question of what might constitute 'effectiveness' in policy formation. Returning to PISA, it is evident that while the data have a utilitarian focus, issues of inequality are not ignored and the charge of reductionism is partly addressed by the broadening of competencies defined as relevant.

Of particular significance here is the OECD Definition and Selection of Key Competencies (DeSeCo) project which has developed and extended the range of competencies in ways that might be regarded as having a broadening rather than a narrowing effect on school curricula (OECD, 2002, 2005b). These include three fundamental competencies: 'the ability to act autonomously', 'using tools inter-actively' and 'functioning in socially heterogeneous groups'. Each of these com-petencies is specified in some detail. For example, the ability to act autonomously includes the ability to form and conduct life plans and personal projects and the ability to defend and assert rights, interests, limits and needs among oth-ers (OECD, 2005b). This commitment to breadth and personal development offers a humanistic discourse, at least on the face of it, which could of course be realised in a variety of ways. To take just one example, in proposed changes to the Scottish school curriculum a complex mix of ideas is evident, including a commitment to individual choice, personalisation, breadth, progression (a single framework to cover the years 3–18) and once again the familiar insistence on the inevitability of change:

> we face new influences.... These include global, social, political and eco-nomic changes, and the particular changes facing Scotland: the need to increase the economic performance of the nation; reflect its growing diver-sity; improve health; and reduce poverty. In addition, we can expect more changes in the patterns and demands of employment, and the likelihood of new and quite different jobs during an individual's working life.
>
> (The Curriculum Review Group, 2004, 10)

The section Why Must the Curriculum Change? raises the issues of technolog-ical change and the importance of connections or partnerships between schools and the wider community as well as connections between schools and other educational institutions – including the sharing of resources. These far-reaching changes are couched in the language of progressive humanism and they suggest many possibilities. It remains to be seen how these will be realised in practice. In Chapter 2, we argued that lifelong learning discourses construct new learner identities and this may be part of the same or similar processes (Chappell *et al.*, 2003). Governmental and international concerns with competitiveness and com-petence have already had transforming affects on all aspects of schooling and will continue to do so. Governments will tackle this in different ways and are likely to introduce widely differing types of policy, these policies will sometimes fail or have unintended consequences. 'Lifelong learning' policies are in this case diverse in their assumptions about what matters and what needs to be done. One often repeated theme, however, is the emphasis on the individual, personal development, personalisation or personalised learning and it is to this focus on the individual that we now turn.

The learner-centred school

The position of the learner in schools is changing for a number of reasons. First, a discourse of learner-centredness emphasising individual choice and flexibility of provision and teaching has exerted a powerful influence on the way that we think about education in general and has become important in policy on schooling in recent years. Second, the growing emphasis on childrens' rights, and changes in social attitudes to schools and education and public sector professionals has changed the social relations in and around schooling. The idea of learner-centredness to the extent that it prioritises the learner's needs and choices promises a progressive and responsive approach to learning and teaching. The implication of this concept and its promotion is that education has historically been far too teacher-centred, that education systems have been too inflexible and that there is a pressing need for reform. The emphasis on learning as opposed to education deliberately shifts attention away from educations systems or provision and towards one that highlights learning processes. Learner-centredness in this context implies choice, provision that facilitates choice and flexible movement of learners through an integrated education system. This clearly implies the need for general reform of those aspects of the education system that limit choice and flexibility. In tertiary education, for example, this has meant offering courses in different modes and in modular form facilitating movement through as well as in and out of the system. For some policy makers this will signify greater marketisation of provision to facilitate choice, or at least greater diversity of provision.

While these ideas have considerable potential to empower learners in making choices, there are some critical points to be made. First, it is not incidental that reforms designed to increase flexibility in tertiary education also increase productivity. In other words, it is possible to meet diverse 'customer' needs in a variety of ways that can in some cases accelerate the process and in most ways intensive workloads for staff. Second, some (see, for example, Bagnall, 2004) have criticised the focus on the individual in education at all levels as individualistic and hence encouraging values of self-interest and individual competition at the expense of community interests. Bagnall (2004) has further criticised the de-emphasis on teaching itself, proposing that responsibility for learning has been privatised and that the role of professional expertise is being ignored. Finally, while it is not inevitable that greater choice and flexibility for learners means a reliance on privatisation and markets, this has been one important aspect of educational reform in some countries. This is controversial because many believe that markets and an emphasis on self-interest discriminate against vulnerable learners. Groups who have traditionally been subject to processes of social exclusion (principally working-class children) may fare at least as badly if not worse in a competitive market.

One example of this focus on the learner in schooling is the current emphasis on personalised learning (PL).[8] In 2004, David Miliband (2006) gave a speech at an international seminar[9] on PL in which he set out his ideas on the importance of choice in schooling. He identified five components of personalized learning, namely

- Assessment for learning, data and dialogue to diagnose every students needs
- Teaching and learning strategies built on individual needs
- Curriculum choice that engages and respects students
- Radical approach to school organisation
- Community, local institutions and social services to support schools.

In addition to the above, Miliband emphasised the importance of school reform, including the need to rethink the way that we organise schools.

These ideas have been expressed as five key components of personalised learning by the DfES in England:

- Effective teaching and learning
- Curriculum entitlement and choice
- School as a learning organisation
- The importance of the world beyond the classroom
- Assessment for learning.

(Pollard and James, 2004)

The notion of personalised learning has become central to debates about the way in which schools might change along a range of different dimensions. It is an incredibly dynamic concept and in the English context is at the time of writing still under development. Leadbetter (2006) notes that the idea has potential to reorganise public services and he offers different models of personalised provision including, for example, bespoke provision, where services are tailored to individual need and mass customisation where learners mix and match elements from existing provision. Other models offered by Leadbetter include a focus on participation and co-creation of value or co-production between participants, such as between teachers and learners; the online encyclopaedia Wikipedia is just one example of this. Leadbetter (2006) also mentions online game communities and eBay. In schools co-creation of value and participation could give children greater voice and participation in learning which might be facilitated by the use of ICT, sharing of experiences and greater access to a wider range of resources and curricula (we discuss different models of using ICT in teaching and learning in Chapter 10). Such changes have the potential to challenge traditional relationships between parents, teachers and pupils and traditional models of school organisation. Even this brief outline of the ideas underlying PL begins to paint a picture of great challenge and change for schools:

A mass, personalised learning service would be revolutionary. By giving learners a growing voice, their aspirations and ambitions would become central to the way that services were organised . . . . Schools would become solution-assemblers, helping children get access to the mix and range of learning resources they need, both virtual and face-to-face. Schools would have to form networks and federations which shared resources and centres of excellence. An individual school in the network would become a gateway to these resources.

(Leadbetter, 2006, 112)

The implications of PL for lifelong learning are not yet clear. Some (Pollard and James, 2004) have expressed doubts about the extent to which issues of learner identities conducive to lifelong participation in learning are addressed by early policy formulations and have called for a rethink of the links between PL and LLL. What is significant about PL is its affinity with a discourse of learner-centredness that has been influential in reforming provision in tertiary education and has been seen as central to the achievement of a learning society. Key elements include choice, flexibility, individual responsibility and personal change. However, PL encompasses other agendas. Like learner-centredness, PL is bound up with political ambitions to reform education. Also – as with the idea of learner-centredness – PL is politically ambiguous and may be supported and deployed by neo-liberal marketisers of public services in addition to those who favour a traditionally strong state which ensures and provides provision for all. One of the key challenges will be the issue of inclusion and equity if changes in the name of PL are to deliver lifelong learners across all social groups.

The connected school

One of the implications of PL is the idea of the networked school; not merely in the sense of being connected to the Internet and shared resources, but in terms of a school's links with other organisations and services. We discuss aspects of networked communities further in Chapter 9. Two aspects of lifelong learning have implications for the relationship between schools and the rest of society. The first of these is the positive impact of the social benefits of learning such as health and well-being, accumulating social capital and the implication, therefore, that curricula should be broad and that schools and communities benefit when they are interlinked. The second aspect is the all-pervasive notion that learning must be flexible in order to engage as many learners as possible. This implies an integrated education system that facilitates the movement of learners from one service or provision to another – a process often characterised by the metaphor of a climbing frame. The following discussion considers possible opportunities for connectivity in contemporary schooling and considers the curriculum, NQFs and community links.

In a discussion of curricula for the future, Young (1998) identifies a range of critical elements in common with learner-centred and personalised learning agendas. For Young, education and learning is increasingly about building links and networks, rather than collecting qualifications. This implies a continuous and lifelong process and one that facilitates student mobility in the education system. Fluidity of content of this kind has the potential to break down distinctions between disciplines and occupations and open up opportunities for co-creation of value or co-production (Leadbetter, 2006). Young refers to this as the *de-differentiated curriculum*, a curriculum that ultimately dissolves divisions between schools and other institutions, education and employment, informal and formal learning and academic and vocational learning. This is congruent with the contemporary PL agenda and with proposals to reform the Scottish school curriculum already discussed at least in theory.[10] It is potentially facilitated by NQFs where levels and credit values of qualifications are nationally and transparently defined and benchmarked, facilitating student mobility between institutions and levels and potentially enhancing access to learning. Here the model is one of flexible and continuous learning. At the same time it is nevertheless one in which outcomes, procedures, criteria for assessment and pre-specification of learning are often rigidly defined and in which discussion of the curriculum often centres more on the procedural, rather than on the actual *content* of learning – which is potentially fluid and constantly changing (Bagnall, 2004; Young, 2003). This model of flexible and continuous learning also has the potential to undercut traditional values about what should or should not be in the curriculum. The implicit assumption is that all knowledge is equal and that hierarchies of 'what really matters' are exclusive and ought to be consigned to the past. This point of view is debatable, but the issue of exactly which values (if any) should be included in the curriculum and exactly what its content should be is an area which has hitherto been underdiscussed except for the expression of concerns that education should not simply be driven by economic imperatives or 'dumbed-down'. Young articulates the former concern, proposing that we should strive for an '. . . education led economy rather than an economy led education . . .' (1998, 155). The de-differentiated curriculum and personalised learning ostensibly could lend themselves equally well to either of these aims.

One aspect of de-differentiation is the growth of NQFs which have become a global phenomenon and are increasingly regarded as central to the creation of a learning society (Young, 2003). It is easy to see why national governments are so keen on them – they help to regulate educational institutions and where this is tied to funding, they provide governments with a measure of control over educational providers.[11] Like PL, NQFs are contradictory or politically ambiguous:

> Much of the discussion about national qualifications frameworks has been concerned with their functions, either as instruments of regulation that provide the basis for controlling the growing and increasingly complex post-compulsory sector or as instruments of communication that enable learners

and employers to be clearer about what different qualifications offer, where they lead and how they are located within the overall system.

(Young, 2003, 233)

Changes in the curricula and the processes of learning thus reveal new possibilities for connectedness, communication and enhanced pupil voice. Yet, at the same time, such changes create possibilities for regulation and wholesale reform of public provision. The public service reform agenda is perhaps particularly apparent in the creation of Community Schools and other variants as well as other examples of integrated services such as Children's Trusts.

Community schools

One initiative which focuses on the social benefits of learning and has the potential to influence learning beyond school in the community and in later life is the concept of the community or full-service school[12] (Smith, 2000, 2004). Such schools were intended to promote positive attitudes to learning, involve parents and communities, support families and encourage children's participation in decision-making (Scottish Office, 1998). These aims have wide-ranging implications for all aspects of schooling, including a greater focus on the individual pupil by means of personalised learning plans, changes in staff development, involvement of a wider range of professionals in schooling and new engagements with local communities. In practical terms, this involves new ways of working and new kinds of services, such as out of school hours childcare, advice and support for parents, an emphasis on inclusive practice, health promoting projects and curricula.

These changes in schools present some challenges. Managing integrated services is complex. Staff development needs may be considerable and there is a risk that individuals and communities may be approached by professionals as 'suitable cases for treatment' rather than genuine partners in change.[13] Nevertheless, the potential benefits of such developments are considerable. Of interest, in relation to lifelong learning is the potential for NCSs and other variants, such as full-service schooling, to generate social capital.[14] In summary, the networks, relationships and reciprocities generated by these developments have the potential to create resources for students, their families and the professionals involved. As we noted, the relationship between social capital and educational attainment is not a straightforward one and it is difficult to demonstrate conclusively that the resources generated by increasing social capital will inevitably lead to higher educational attainment. Nevertheless, such developments have the capacity to increase civil engagement in communities and individuals who are civically engaged are most likely to value LLL (Field, 1999, 2005). Moreover, Remedios and Allan (2006) note that the connectedness fostered by NCS developments in Scotland appears to have positive affective outcomes, including increasing empathy, trust and reciprocity. These affective outcomes may be just as important in achieving change in individuals and communities as 'official' outcomes such as improved attainment:

> we believe we observed individuals changing their direction and purpose. In this sense we believe that the journey towards trying to achieve tangible outcomes can often create useful outcomes on the way. It may be that achieving a degree of connectedness may be as (or more) important than the targeted outcomes.
>
> (Remedios and Allan, 2006, 624)

In summary, moves towards the creation of a learning society and other imperatives not explored here, such as increasing the emphasis on children's rights and on improving the quality of children's lives via, for example, the expansion and co-ordination of services for children, are likely to mean that schools will become progressively integrated into communities, wider education systems and indeed into other elements of public services. This new connectedness may be realised in practice in different ways and the examples explored here are not necessarily representative of all of the many possibilities that exist. These possibilities are contingent upon a number of factors – to take just one example, governments will vary in the extent to which they will allow the market to play a part in achieving the 'connected school' (e.g. private finance, local business involvement, etc.). However connectivity is achieved; it is likely to mean that all aspects of schooling will continue to change considerably in coming years.

Schooling and lifelong learning in the future

The common themes identified here which link new policies and practices in schooling with lifelong learning such as connectedness or connectivity and learner-centredness are likely to have diverse implications in practice. In its *Schooling for Tomorrow* series, the OECD (2001) identifies three broad possibilities for the future of schools. These are *the status quo extrapolated* (in which existing models are strengthened), *re-schooling* (in which systems are given new direction and purpose) and finally *de-schooling* (in which there is a decline in the importance of schools altogether) (p. 78). These three possibilities are further broken down into six possible scenarios. These are the following:

1. Robust bureaucratic systems
2. Extending the market model
3. Schools as core social centres
4. Schools as focused learning organizations
5. Learner networks and the network society
6. Teacher exodus The Meltdown scenario.

(OECD, 2001)

In the event that the status quo is preserved, two models are offered. The first of these is described as one whereby schools are represented as strongly bureaucratic systems resistant to change. In the second model, there is an emphasis on markets rather than bureaucracy, which, potentially at least, offer greater choice and diversity of provision, the involvement of business and closer links to entrepreneurship and the labour market. One of the risks associated with this scenario might be an increase in inequalities and exclusion. Alternative situations are also modelled in the case of re-schooling. The first of these would include the NCSs such as those in Scotland. According to this model, schools would have the potential to become core social centres and centres of social capital formation, giving them a wide remit and focusing on the widest possible definition of the benefits of learning. This does present considerable challenges at every level, however. Moreover, the nature of the types of partnerships formed is crucial, as we note in Chapter 8. Communities may be empowered to set their own agendas or at the other extreme, approached by professionals as 'suitable cases for treatment'. Also, linking schools with local communities might serve to reflect or even reinforce the inequalities which inevitably persist – to whatever extent – within and between communities. A more limited model might present schools as networked organisations within the education system, as learning organisations play a leading role in promoting the ethos of lifelong learning. Lifelong learning discourses are not neutral, of course. They are diverse, potentially contradictory and constantly changing and have the power to generate significant social change in a number of directions. Change will inevitably be controversial.

Finally, in the case of the de-schooling theory, two models are offered. The first of these envisages a move away from the centrality of schools as institutions facilitated by ICT and a more networked society. Diverse learning networks over distances would replace schools. Again, the problem of the exclusion of particular social groups may be difficult to address in such a model. Second, it might be argued that one of the key roles of schools is the contribution they make to fostering community and collectivity and that this aim would be undermined in this model. In the final scenario offered by the OECD, teacher shortage is projected to result in a complete rethink of schooling, with possible conflict over solutions leading either to considerable change or retrenchment and the possible decline of schools.

Lifelong learning agendas are not simply about learning in 'later life'. They have multiple objectives. They are complex and varied and disentangling some of these agendas will be challenging, to say the least. Additionally, the implications of these agendas for schools are profound and this will add a sense of urgency to the debate. These implications include the following: a re-evaluation of curricula and processes of learning and potentially greater fluidity in both; a focus on individual learners and a concern with personal development and change; and greater connectivity between schools, the rest of the education system and communities. Finally, the aim to reform public services also includes schooling and is likely to have implications for school organisation, staffing and community engagement.

Notes

1 See Reay (2006) for a useful overview of the contemporary relevance of social class in schooling. See also Ball, 2003; Archer, Hutchings and Ross, 2003 on class and inclusion/exclusion in compulsory and post-compulsory education.

2 We do not argue here that these concerns with inequality are less relevant today. Indeed on the issue of class inequalities in schooling, there is evidence that these are extremely entrenched and arguably a central concern for any aspirations towards the learning society. See Reay (2006) on the persistence of class inequalities in schools. Nevertheless, in this chapter we focus on the challenges presented by contemporary lifelong learning policies and discourses.

3 There are 30 OECD countries, namely Australia, Austria, Belgium, Canada, Czech Republic, Denmark, Finland, France, Germany, Greece, Hungary, Iceland, Ireland, Italy, Korea, Japan, Luxembourg, Mexico, Netherlands, New Zealand, Norway, Portugal, Poland, Slovak Republic, Spain, Sweden, Switzerland, Turkey, UK, and US.

4 It is of interest that a survey of parents and teenagers by the Learning and Skills Network found that only 50.5 per cent of teenagers supported such a change. Adults were more supportive (71.2 per cent). Interestingly, the group least likely to support the proposals amongst adults were middle-class parents – 30 per cent of them disagree with the proposals and 65 per cent agree (Villeneuve-Smith, Marshall and Munoz, 2007).

5 This is defined by PISA as the '. . . capacity of students to analyse, reason and communicate effectively as they pose, solve and interpret mathematical problems . . . '(OECD, 2006, 63).

6 These two are Finland and Korea.

7 This is defined as the length of time a five-year-old can be expected to be enrolled in education during lifetime.

8 At the time of writing, the Department for Education and Skills in England had devoted a website to the promotion of personalised learning, which may be accessed at the following URL: http://www.standards.dfes.gov.uk/personalisedlearning/.

9 This was jointly organised by the English DfES and the OECD. David Miliband was then Minister for School Standards.

10 In practice, the implications of the de-differentiated curriculum are potentially contradictory. National qualification frameworks, when tied to funding, give governments a large measure of control over the curriculum. Governments will also differ in the extent to which the contents of a national curriculum are specified.

11 Young (2003) distinguishes between strong and weak frameworks but this is a difficult distinction to make. As long as frameworks are tied to funding, a myriad of possible constraints on individual institutions become possible.

12 Typically, community schools include a range of services, links with the communities often via parents and other social or public health agendas such as integration of health promotion in the curriculum. New Community Schools (NCS) are specific to Scotland, but also of relevance here is the creation of Children's Trusts in England which have the aim of unifying children's services in order to implement legislation designed to improve children's services such as the 2004 Children Act. See DfES (2005) for an assessment of Children's Trusts. See also UNICEF (2007).

13 This idea is discussed in more depth in Chapter 8.

14 Social capital theories are discussed fully in Chapter 3.

References

Archer, L., Hutchings, M. and Ross, A. (2003) *Higher Education and Social Class: Issues of Exclusion and Inclusion*. London: RoutledgeFalmer.

Bagnall, R. (2004) *Cautionary Tales in the Ethics of Lifelong Learning Policy and Management: A Book of Fables*. London: Kluwer Academic Publishers.

Ball, S.J. (1998) Educational studies: Policy entrepreneurship and social theory. In Slee, R., Weiner, G. and Tomlinson, S. (eds) *School Effectiveness for Whom? Challenges to the School Effectiveness and School Improvement Movements*. London: Falmer Press.

Ball, S. (2003) *Class Strategies and the Education Market: The Middle Classes and Social Advantage*. London: Routledge.

Ball, S. (2006) *Education Policy and Social Class, The Selected Works of Stephen J Ball*. London: RoutledgeFalmer.

Brown (1998) The tyranny of the international horse race. In Slee, R., Weiner, G. and Tomlinson, S. (eds) *School Effectiveness for Whom? Challenges to the School Effectiveness and School Improvement Movements*. London: Falmer Press.

Chappell, C., Rhodes, C., Soloman, N., Tennant, M. and Yates, L. (2003) *Reconstructing the Lifelong Learner: Pedagogy and Identity in Individual, Organisational and Social Change*. London: Routledge.

Department for Education and Skills (DfES) (2004) *The Children Act*. London: HMSO.

Department for Education and Skills (DfES) (2005) *Children's Trusts: Developing Integrated Services for Children in England*. National Evaluation of Children's Trusts, Phase 1. Interim Report University of East Anglia in Association with the National Children's Bureau Research Report RR617. London: HMSO.

Department for Education and Skills (DfES) (2007) *Raising Expectations: Staying in Education and Training Post-16*. London: HMSO.

Field, J. (1999) Schooling, networks and the labour market: Explaining participation in Northern Ireland. *British Educational Research Journal* 25(4): 501–516.

Field, J. (2005) *Social Capital and Lifelong Learning*. Bristol: Policy Press.

Gask, K. (2006) Population review of 2004 and 2005: England and Wales. *Population Trends*, 126 Winter, 8–15, London: HMSO.

Instance, D. (2003) Schooling and lifelong learning: Insights from OECD analyses. *European Journal of Education Research Development and Policies*, 38(1).

Kelly, A.V. (1999) *The Curriculum: Theory and Practice*, 4th Edition. London: Paul Chapman.

Leadbetter, C. (2006) The future of public services: Personalised learning. *Personalising Learning*. Paris: OECD.

Lingard, B., Ladwig, J. and Luke, A. (1998) School effects in postmodern conditions. In Slee, R. and Weiner, G., and Tomlinson, S. (eds) *School Effectiveness for Whom? Challenges to the School Effectiveness and School Improvement Movements*. London: Falmer Press.

Miliband, D. (2006) Choice and Voice in Personalised Learning. *Personalising Education*. Paris: OECD.

Organisation for Economic Co-operation and Development (OECD) (2001) *What Schools for the Future? Schooling for Tomorrow*. Paris: OECD.

Organisation for Economic Co-operation and Development (OECD) (2002) *Definition and selection of key competencies: Theoretical and conceptual foundations*. Strategy Paper. Paris: OECD.

Organisation for Economic Co-operation and Development (OECD) (2005a) *Education Policy Analysis 2004*. Paris: OECD.

Organisation for Economic Co-operation and Development (OECD) (2005b) *Definition and Selection of Key Competencies*. Paris: OECD.

Organisation for Economic Co-operation and Development (OECD) (2006) *Education At a Glance OECD Indicators 2006*. Paris: OECD.

Pollard, A. and James, M. (eds) *Personalised Learning: A Commentary by the Teaching and Learning Research Programme*. London: TLRP and ESRC.

Reay, D. (2006) The zombie stalking English schools: Social class and educational inequality. *British Journal of Educational Studies*, 54(3): 288–307.

Remedios, R. and Allan, J. (2006) New community schools and the measurement of transformation. *International Journal of Inclusive Education*. 10(6): 615–625.

Schuller, T., Hammond, C., Bassett-Grundy, A., Preston, J. and Bynner, J. (2004) *The Benefits of Learning, The Impact of Education on Health, Family Life and Social Capital*. London: Routledge.

Slee, R. and Weiner, G. (1998) Introduction: School effectiveness for Whom. In Slee, R., Weiner, G. and Tomlinson, S. (eds) *School Effectiveness for Whom? Challenges to the School Effectiveness and School Improvement Movements*. London: Falmer Press.

Slee, R., Weiner, G. and Tomlinson, S. (1998) *School Effectiveness for Whom? Challenges to the School Effectiveness and School Improvement Movements*. London: Falmer Press.

Smith, M.K. (2000, 2004) Full-service schooling. *The Encyclopaedia of Informal Education*, at http://www.infed.org/schooling/f-serv.htm (accessed February 2007).

The Curriculum Review Group (2004) *A Curriculum for Excellence*. Edinburgh: Scottish Executive, available at http://www.scotland.gov.uk/Publications/2004/11/20178/45862 (accessed June 2007).

The Scottish Office (1998) *New Community Schools Prospectus*. Edinburgh: The Scottish Office, at http://www.scotland.gov.uk/library/documents-w3/ncsp-00.htm (accessed March 2007).

UNICEF Innocenti Research Centre (2007) *An Overview of Child Well-being in Rich Countries*. A comprehensive assessment of the lives and well-being of children and adolescents in the economically advanced nations, Innocenti Report Card 7, Florence: United Nations Children's Fund.

Villeneuve-Smith, F., Marshall, L. and Munoz, S. (2007) *Raising the School Leaving Age: Are the public convinced? A Survey of Parents and Teenagers*. London: Learning and Skills Network.

Young, M.F.D. (1998) *The Curriculum of the Future: From the 'New Sociology of Education' to a Critical Theory of Learning*. London: Falmer Press.

Young, M.F.D. (2003) National qualifications frameworks as a global phenomenon: A comparative perspective. *Journal of Education and Work*. 16(30): 223–237.

Chapter 6

Lifelong learning and formal post-compulsory education

An entire chapter could be devoted to defining what we mean by term *formal post-compulsory education*.[1] Broadly, the territory in institutional terms is, on the one hand, universities and other institutions that offer largely Higher Education (HE) provision, and, on the other, colleges that offer less advanced and largely Vocational Education and Training (VET). Such distinctions are of course approximations since in reality there exist a continuum of forms of institutions across the world, some offering a mix of levels of educational offers. Our focus in this chapter is the HE sector and its accessibility for lifelong learners, and we focus in particular on widening participation to universities, and as a consequence we will also consider the role of colleges that offer VET in this context. The International Standard Classification of Education (ISCED) makes a further distinction between types of educational provision which classifies education by orientation and level. In this scheme programmes are classified as either type A, being of a largely theoretical nature, or type B, having a largely occupational orientation. In terms of level, ISCED distinguishes between Level 4 (post-secondary non-tertiary education), Level 5 (the first stage of tertiary education, also known as short cycle HE) and Level 6 (the second stage of tertiary education leading to research degrees).

If we look around the world, however, we see much blurring across these three ways of categorising (type of institution, orientation of provision and level of study). Most potential for confusion lies in the use of the term *Higher Education*, which can refer to the level of provision (ISCED 5 and 6) and to the type of institution (a Higher Education Institution (HEI) often, but not always, titled a university). HE is largely what HEIs do, but not exclusively: in particular this caveat applies in the area of lifelong learning since some institutions may, for example, offer pre-university preparatory used to widen access and non-credit continuing education directed towards older adults studying largely for personal development. But other institutions that are not HEIs also offer HE (as well as provision at ISCED level 4 and lower), notable examples being Technical and Further Education Colleges (TAFE) in Australia (see Wheelahan and Moodie, 2005) and the Further Education Colleges (FECs) of the UK, which offer significant proportions of first cycle HE. These institutions have in

Scotland been major contributors to the expansion of total HE provision (see Gallacher, 2005).

It is also important to recognise that there are many variations in practice from country to country. In some countries by definition HE is defined as type A provision irrespective of provider (e.g. Finland and Greece); in others there exist parallel type A and B provision up to Masters level (e.g. Poland and Estonia)[2]. Provision at the ISCED level 4 is very diverse and perhaps is best summarised by what it is not, namely compulsory school provision or tertiary education. Alternatively it can be classified in terms of three forms: general education; pre-vocational or pre-technical education; vocational or technical education. Institutionally it is found in a range of types of institutions, the generic term VET college often being used to describe one set of providers, and this encompasses a range of designations internationally.

As has already become evident, there is little homogeneity within this domain and nor is there within categories of institution. National HEIs systems and the type of institutions contained with these systems have been subject to considerable analysis in terms of their distinguishing features. Perhaps the most well-known form of differentiation of HEIs is that described by Scott (1995, 35) who proposes that HEIs can be classified as *dual, binary, unified* and *stratified*. In this model both dual and binary systems contain alternative forms of HE providers; such systems offer comparable, but distinguishable forms of provision and in the case of the binary model, alternative institutions have been set up to complement and rival existing traditional structures. Examples include the binary system of universities and *ammattikorkeakoulu* (polytechnics) in Finland, Institutes of Technology in Ireland and *Fachhochschulen* (universities of applied sciences) in Germany, the distinction in each case being between type A and B orientation. In unified systems in principal there is no formal differentiation of institutions, all of which have the same status. Often this has been the result of legislation to remove differentiation such as in the UK (between universities and polytechnics) and Australia (between universities and colleges of advanced education). Systems said to be stratified allocate different institutions a specific role within a total system. Most notable in this respect are the community colleges of the US and Canada, and to an increasing degree the FECs of the UK, all of which offer short cycle HE (amongst other provision at a lower level in most cases) which may articulate to longer programmes of HE in other institutions.

Martin Trow's (2005) functional model of HE systems describes systems as either elite (with less than 15 per cent of school-leavers enrolled), mass (15–40 per cent of this age group) or universal (40 per cent). He argues that the function of institutions within elite systems is to shape the mind and character of a ruling class; prepare them for elite roles, citing examples that include the German *Humboldtian* model placing graduate study and research as its first priority, the *Grande Ecoles* of France providing professional workers, and historically, the 'personality model' of Oxford and Cambridge in the UK 'civilising our gentlemen' and initiating them into a liberal intellectual culture. A mass system has the function of transmission of skills and preparation for a broader range of technical and economic elite roles and has been described as the 'University as service station'. Finally, the universal system is linked to the adaptation of the 'whole population' to rapid social and technological change. It is important to emphasise here that the differences between these types cannot simply be understood in terms of numbers of students participating. The differences are more complex. In the mass and universal models, there is a new emphasis on performance and producing workers for the knowledge economy, for example. Citing Lyotard (1984), Edwards and Usher (2000) argue that the expansion of higher education amounts to,

> the creation of a market for competence in operational skills . . . students will no longer predominantly be young people from the liberal elite seeking a liberal education – a training in civility and sensibility – or an education appropriate to the traditional elite professions – a training in rationality. (p. 77)

Trow's categorisation has been subject to criticism as being descriptive, deterministic and linear (Gellert and Teichler 1993 and Teichler 1998), but as Brennan (2004) points out,

> Trow never saw these distinctions as empirical descriptions of real higher education systems, rather as models or 'ideal types' to aid our comprehension of such systems. And a further point to remember is that although he saw these forms as sequential stages, he did not regard it as inevitable that the later stages would completely replace the earlier ones. In particular, he saw definite possibilities of examples of elite forms surviving in the mass and universal stages.
>
> (p. 24)

The main helpfulness of these broad distinctions is that they help us locate particular institutions in a typology that relates to a broad underlying mission as it pertains to lifelong learners. It is therefore a useful starting point for considering the impact of lifelong learning policies and discourses on higher education itself as well as changes in the student body and the student experience. They alert us to two key aspects of changes. First, there is the phenomenal expansion of participation in higher education which includes at least a commitment to widening participation to previously excluded groups. Second, there is an increasing emphasis on performance (the efficient production of graduates for the knowledge economy), flexibility and accountability. These new demands on institutions are realised via funding mechanisms, inter-institutional competition and NQFs. Such policy levers have produced a galvanising discourse of 'accessibility' and a range of policies designed to widen access to higher education to previously excluded groups. These in turn have produced a wide range of institutional responses.

Widening participation

The need for greater equity of access to tertiary level provision is one of the principal concerns in many societies. Expansions of the HE systems of many countries around the world in the last three decades have occurred with three main concerns in mind: social justice, demographic trends and economic development. McGivney (1990) suggested that these have been the three major imperatives for policies that have sought to increase and widen access for adult students, and they are now applicable to initiatives directed across population seeking entry to HE.

These three policy drivers were also highlighted by Gallacher, Osborne and Postle (1996) in their comparative study of Australia and Scotland. They analyse, 'how educational systems systematically disadvantage certain social groups', and that as a consequence 'measures are required to encourage wider participation from these groups for reasons of equity and social justice'. Second, they identify that 'access is encouraged for reasons associated with pragmatism and expediency at times when patterns of demographic decline amongst high school leavers indicate a need to find new sources of recruits to higher education'. Third, they show how national self-interest relates to arguments put forward by government that 'investment in human capital is important for the economic growth and development of society, and that increased access will help sustain economic competitiveness with international rivals'.

A number of activities can be identified which are centred around the theme of *social justice*. These tend to focus on providing 'second chances' for groups who gained relatively little from education at school level, and the target groups tend to be those from the lowest socio-economic groups and from areas with the highest levels of social and economic deprivation. In the UK, from the late 1970s until the present day, there has been provision of this type offered directly by most universities or in collaboration with FECs. Many of these *Access Courses* involve a range of other stakeholders, including local authorities, and have assumed a strong regional dimension (see, for example, SHEFC, 2000), the rationale being that effectiveness of initiatives requires collaboration between different stakeholders and that this is more easily facilitated at local level. A range of consortia arrangements have been developed over the years within the aegis, amongst others, of Open College Networks, Aim Higher Partnerships and Lifelong Learning Networks.[3] There are echoes here of the 'learning region' approach described in Chapter 9. In the UK for universities, this activity is clearly one part of what is often described as the 'Third Mission' of engagement with local communities (see Floud, 2001), and evokes historical traditions of democracy found within a strand of activity once known as 'liberal adult education'.[4]

It is, however, important to note that over time in the UK the principal target groups has changed radically, with emphasis in the last decade shifting from adults to disadvantaged young people, and that leads us to the second of McGivney's reasons underlying widening participation to HE. In the UK, the emphasis on adult participation during the 1980s arose from concern about the implications of the *demographic* trends, which produced predictions that by the mid-1990s there would be significant reductions in the number of school pupils progressing to HE. Although by the late 1980s and early 1990s, it had been established that these forecasts were exaggerated, concerns over the implications of demographic decline were a significant factor in influencing both national policy and some institutional policy, particularly in discipline areas where recruitment has traditionally been more difficult such as science and engineering. However, when in the late 1990s the challenges presented by global competition became even more significant than in earlier decades, a focus on the second chance beyond school was considered an insufficient response to challenges that lay ahead. The majority of current UK access initiatives (see Thomas *et al.*, 2005) are concerned with early intervention and awareness raising. Whilst these activities still seek to target the most disadvantages (as measured by socio-economic status), there is no doubt a parallel economic rationale that it's cheaper to intervene early as found in some of the arguments in Chapter 4 concerned with the economics of lifelong learning.

Therefore, since the 1980s a (if not the) major imperative of the UK government in increasing participation to higher education have been concerned with the *economic development* of the country. By the second half of the 1980s, the view amongst policy makers was that the HE system was unsuited to plans for economic growth and compared badly with many of the UK's international competitors. By the 1990s, the increasing emphasis on global competition and the need for countries to improve the skill levels in the population had become central features of lifelong learning policies. These were increasingly combined with concerns about equality of opportunity in the race to expand participation. Such considerations were principal reasons for a series of initiatives from that time to the present day, which have sought to widen access to higher education and move towards a mass system of higher education rather than the elite system which had existed. Two Education White Papers (DFES, 1987,1991) emphasised the importance of widening access to *vocationally* relevant education, and the theme of the economic outcomes of education was reiterated in the White Paper *Competitiveness: Forging Ahead* (HMSO, 1995), which emphasises individual responsibility for vocational lifetime learning. Later, the Dearing and Garrick reports (NCIHE, 1997) offered a vision of a learning society which embraces people at all levels of achievement, and envisaged the expansion of HE with particular emphasis on short-cycle level courses. A number of British Green Papers (DfEE, 1998; SOEID, 1998; WO, 1998) built on this report and echoed many of the themes found in the European White Paper *Teaching and Learning: Towards the Learning Society* (EC, 1995) with the concern that it had expressed about the impact of the information society, internationalisation and development in science and technology.

We have been closely concerned with this issue for a number of decades, and a number of other publications have discussed and analysed policies and practices around the world (Morgan-Klein and Murphy, 2002; Osborne, 2003a and b; Osborne, Gallacher and Crossan, 2004; Thomas *et al.*, 2005). In work that we carried out in the early part of this decade we sought to classify the range of interventions that exist around the world with the aim of improving the access of groups that traditionally do not participate in HE. These include those from lower social economic groups and certain ethnic minorities, individuals in geographically remote areas, people with physical disabilities and in certain disciplines, women. Our categorisation of widening participation is threefold: *in-reach*, *out-reach* and *flexibility*. In-reach refers to activity which seeks to improve supply to existing provision in HE, but providing new forms of access. By contrast out-reach refers to collaboration with external partners, and seeks to be responsive to demand and create new demands from populations who may not have previously considered HE. Flexibility refers to initiatives that involve structural modification of systems that make them more accessible and may also be accompanied by collaboration.

In-reach might be viewed as those activities that occur within terms set by HEIs, namely initiatives that provide access to that which already exists. It has been argued that many actions within this category do not challenge the limitations of the existing offer in HE and simply remediate its deficiencies (see Murphy *et al.*, 2002). The aforementioned Access Courses for adults are included in this category and so too are special entry tests for both school-leavers and adults such as the French Special University Entrance Examination (*Examen Spécial d'Entrée à l'Universit* (l'ESEU)), later the *Diplôme d'Accès aux Etudes Universitaires* (DAEU) for adults who do not complete the *Baccalauréat* at school (Davies, 1999) and the Spanish *Prueba de acceso a la universidad para mayores de 25 años* (Ortega and Camara, 2001). These forms of 'second chance' are content-based and to a large extent replications of traditional school-leaving examinations and do not take into account the particular needs of adults (Bourgeois and Frenay, 2001).

Other tests of a different type seek to find a culturally non-specific measure of ability as a supplement to academic grades achieved through traditional testing at school. This has become necessary both in the UK and Australia where demand for places in some disciplines such as Medicine far outstrips supply and where there appears to be inequity in access. Admission to Medicine in the UK is skewed heavily towards higher social economic groups, and although in part this is a function of differentially high application rates by these groups (see Thomas *et al.*, 2005), there clearly are issues of equity in selection to be addressed (see McGavock and Osborne, 2005). Instruments akin to the US Scholastic Ability Tests (SATs) including psychometric tests such as the Personal Quality Assessment (PQA) and the Bio Medical Admissions Test (BMAT) have been developed to aid selection of candidates with predicted 'A' grades at General Certificate of Education GCE A level. One of the main reasons for using the tests is to measure aptitudes that cannot be coached and so assess ability in a way that is independent of social class. Psychometric tests are still being piloted, but are being increasingly used in selection procedures, and as of 2006 the UK Clinical

Aptitude Test (UKCAT) has been used as part of the selection process to medical schools in the UK. More generally, the Sutton Trust has proposed the piloting of a US-style SATs as a potential common test for use in the UK (see McDonald, Newton and Whetton, 2001), and the Schwartz Report on *Fair Admissions to Higher Education* (DfES, 2004, p. 11) has reported that if 'proposed research concludes that a national test of potential would offer significant benefits, the Steering Group urges the Government to grasp this opportunity as it takes forward the Tomlinson proposals' for curriculum reform.

There are many initiatives that seek to widening participation through out-reach activities. Rather than a second chance, much provision in this arena is a *First Chance* for those groups who have been traditionally excluded from HE. Strategies that better facilitate direct entry from a particular sector to HE, as is exemplified in the links between VET colleges and universities in the UK (Morgan-Klein, 2003; Morgan-Klein and Murphy, 2002). Various models of workplace learning (Brennan and Little, 1996) are also clear examples of this type of work. Similar links between first cycle and second cycle HE exist in other countries such as Australia, Canada and the US. In some states in Australia, a further stage of development has occurred in which TAFE colleges and univer-sities have been integrated to form a common post-16 dual-mode system (see Wheelahan and Moodie, 2005).

Flexibility

The third category of access initiative is that of flexibility. The concept of flex-ibility has been used in a variety of ways and raises a number of issues. (see Harrison *et al.*, 2003; Nicoll, 2006). At one level flexibility is represented as an imperative for individuals to maintain their economic competitiveness. As we noted in Chapter 1, in terms of lifelong learning generally, flexibility has been an integral component of the rhetoric found in a range of policy statements. Here we are concerned with the structure of provision and its relationship to individual and organisation need. The following quote from the Green Paper *Opportunity Scotland: A Paper on Lifelong Learning* is illustrative of the system level dimension of flexibility:

> Qualifications today must reflect needs for certificated learning which are far more varied than ever before. The key to this will be a structure of qual-ifications which is flexible enough to meet individual and employer needs, provides easily understood opportunities and pathways and offers standards recognised and valued by everyone. Learning needs vary and people require access to education at different stages in their lives. Flexibility must be a feature of the system if individuals are to be encouraged back into learning and continue to build up qualifications over longer periods of time, perhaps through part-time or work-based learning.
>
> (SOEID, 1998, para 14.3)

This concern with flexibility is not unique to the UK. The recent London Communiqué, which has reviewed progress in establishing the European Higher Education Area (EHEA)[5] speaks of the objective of a student-centred higher education, and bemoans that its 'stocktaking report shows that some elements of flexible learning exist in most countries, but a more systematic development of flexible learning paths to support lifelong learning is at an early stage' (Bologna Secretariat, 2007, p.3).

In the field of widening participation, from the demand-side, flexibility relates to issues of structure, space and time. It refers to organisational modifications that are intended to fit in with students' personal circumstances. Thus flexibility may be manifested in modular, part-time, distance and ICT-mediated programmes, and sometimes courses that contain a number of these characteristics. Modularity refers to the means by which teaching and learning are packaged into discrete episodes, and often associated with credit that can be accumulated in a way that is independent of time and to a lesser extent institution. National Qualification Frameworks[6] and Credit Accumulation and Transfer Systems (CATS) provide the structural bases for these mechanisms since they are the templates against which credit is mapped. An 'ideal' (or extreme) scenario is such a world would be one where credit can be achieved in a multiplicity of sites (e.g. home, workplace, VET college, HEI), modes (part-time, full-time), times (e.g. daytime, evening, weekend, summer) and technologies. It is worth noting that the constraints of time and space do not disappear. For example, students' domestic circumstances will vary and this will mean that the experience of 'managing' such flexibility will vary across social groups. It may be highly gendered, for example (we refer to this in Chapter 2). Credit becomes the unifying currency for this flexibility. Whilst there are merits in creating the conditions that allow an individual to construct such learning paths, questions must be asked as to *what* is learned in such scenarios given what would inevitably be the discontinuous nature of such an experience. The flip side of flexibility is a potentially dislocated learning experience within which reflective development is downgraded. Moreover, credit transfer and accreditation of prior learning may mean that it is also an accelerated experience. Pressures at institutional and individual level to *condense* learning raise questions about quality and purpose. That being said, many traditional systems create barriers simply by taking a 'one size that must fit all' approach. This clearly excludes many individuals who by virtue of their location, job or other situational factors cannot participate as full-time day students. It is worth emphasising again here the mix of social and economic concerns in the widening participation agenda. On the one hand, there is a humanistic concern with student needs and experience and a focus on social justice in accessibility discourses. On the other hand, there is a utilitarian emphasis on economic imperatives and producing more graduates in a competitive and efficient manner. These are brought together in a discourse of flexibility which is deployed in ways that emphasise accessibility and student-centredness and at the same time bring increased competition, accelerated learning and downward pressure on resources as institutions compete.

In Chapter 10, we consider information and communication technologies (ICTs) and we can expect the flexibility offered by the rapid and increasing availability (and decreasing cost) of a variety of ways to access learning through such means to radically change opportunities in the future. Distance education universities using earlier low levels of technology have for some decades offered a way to combat lack of educational opportunity for reasons including of geographical location, disability (CEDEFOP, 2001), and employment and home circumstances. Now and in future decades, the flexibility discourse within lifelong learning, of meeting students' needs at times and places of their own choosing, would seem most readily achievable through ICTs. After over a decade of false dawns within which pedagogical promise has outshone technological capability and cost, it now appears that robust and reliable broadband services at accessible prices are available to offer, at least in the more affluent OECD countries. Early technological failings and the cost of access to telephony had led to a lack of confidence in the potential of ICT.

Finally, flexibility in provision may also challenge constructions of what constitutes valid knowledge and the means by which knowledge can be acquired and demonstrated such as the recognition and accreditation of prior (experiential) learning (R/AP(E)L) described in Chapter 7. This also includes programmes of independent study, within which students are able to negotiate the content of the curriculum (see Percy and Ramsden, 1980).

Concluding remarks

Our focus in this chapter has been HE and widening participation, and consciously we have excluded the other contributions that this sector makes to lifelong learning. In another text (Osborne and Thomas, 2003), one of us has dealt with the panoply of provision offered within the aegis of University Continuing Education (UCE) in Europe, which includes a range of provision that broadly can be described as either Continuing Personal Education (CPE) or Continuing Professional Development (CPD). Like the distinction between the social and the economic, this is a blurred categorisation that expresses how directly a programme links to current or future employment, and space does not allow us to focus on the detail. One trend that we certainly see in the UK, and beyond Europe in Canada and the US has been a move away from what has been described as the 'Wisconsin model'(Gooch, 1995) of university extension with its focus on serving local and regional communities[7] to one which emphasises a market-oriented UCE offering CPD and other full-cost recovery courses.

The focus on widening participation that we have chosen in this chapter has allowed us to emphasise one of the activities of universities that most closely relates to core social concerns of lifelong learning in the modern age. Access to mainstream university provision has been rationed historically, and the credentials that such access provides are powerful in creating greater social and economic opportunity. In Chapter 4, we stress that there are many caveats in relation to the benefits that pertain from achieving qualifications, but there is no doubt that for most individuals that these are considerable.

We also recognise that there is a huge literature concerned with the student experience in HE, and in relation to *what* is learned. Pascarella and Terenzini (1991 and 2005) provide impressive reviews of the field, especially from a US perspective, where considerable attention is given to institutional research, and Brennan and Jary (2005) offer a UK perspective. It certainly is the case that the story does not stop at the point of access.

The terrain of HE will of course no doubt change in the future, and will be subject to increasing global influences. Enders *et al.* (2005) have projected three futures for 2020 using the metaphors of *Centralia* (the City of the Sun), *Octavia* (the Spider-web City) and *Vitis Vinifera* (the City of Traders and Micro-climates) for universities in Europe. The first scenario is characterised as strong hierarchical coordination, with power centralised in the European Commission ('the muscles from Brussels'); the second envisages strong networking as its central concept with a variety of links between organisations and actors on the supply and demand side; and the third scenario is that of a market scenario, in which competition between suppliers dominates. We must hope that whatever the future brings, that social purpose and the 'third mission' maintain a foothold in the university offer.

Notes

1 See Osborne (2005) for a discussion of the various forms of education beyond compulsory schooling.
2 Many other variants could be described, for those interested in such issues we recommend EURYDICE (2003).
3 See http://www.nocn.org.uk/ for details of Open College Networks. For details of the Aimhigher programme, see http://www.aimhigher.ac.uk/home/index.cfm and the Lifelong Learning Networks (LLNs), http://www.hefce.ac.uk/widen/lln/. The LLNs are complementary to the work of the Aimhigher programme, which principally aims to raise aspirations and attainment to widen access and participation into HE. The focus of LLNs is on improving progression opportunities for vocational learners into and through higher education.
4 For overviews of the historic roles of universities in the field of continuing education see Fieldhouse (1996), and for a more recent overview of the third mission see Osborne and Thomas (2003). We have already alluded to these and other traditions in Chapter 3.
5 One of the principal objects of the Bologna Process started in 1999 is harmonisation of higher education systems across Europe within the EHEA and some 45 countries are involved. It is described as a process within which student choice, transparency of qualifications and mutual recognition of qualifications is paramount. Further, it is explicitly seen to be a factor for Europe to be able to compete economically with the US and Asia. In the 2007 Stocktaking Report (see http://www.dfes.gov.uk/bologna/uploads/documents/6909-BolognaProcessST.pdf) each of these countries has a 'Bologna Scorecard' against 12 indicators of progress on a 5-point scale.
6 National Qualifications Frameworks are descriptions of the achievements represented by higher education qualifications in a series of levels. For example, in England there

are five levels within which bands of qualifications said to share similar outcomes (see http://www.qaa.ac.uk/academicinfrastructure/FHEQ/EWNI/default.asp).   Many other countries have such frameworks, including Australia and New Zealand. A European Qualifications Framework is being implemented by the European Union under the aegis of the Lisbon Agenda (http://ec.europa.eu/education/policies/ educ/eqf/index_en.html) and is seen as another arm within the objective of securing transparency of qualifications and mobility of labour.

7 See   http://www.library.wisc.edu/etext/WIReader/Contents/Idea.html   for McCarthy's (1912) original ideas. His Wisconsin model involved the highest ranking professors working within the community, a focus on the practical application of knowledge especially to the agricultural community and dedicated funding for provision by the state. The model was replicated across North America and parallel some early traditions in the UK as described by Fieldhouse (1996).

References

Bologna Secretariat (2007) *Towards the European Higher Education Area: Responding to Challenges in a Globalised World – The London Communiqué*, at http://www.dfes.gov. uk/bologna/uploads/documents/LC18May07.pdf

Bourgeois, E. and Frenay, M. (2001) *University Adult Access Policies and Practices across the European Union; and Their Consequences for the Participation of Non-traditional Adults*. Final Report to European Commission of TSER Project, SOE2-CT97-2021.

Brennan, J. (2004) The social role of the contemporary university: Contradictions, boundaries and change. *Ten Years On: Changing Education in a Changing World*. Milton Keynes: Centre for Higher Education Research and Information, The Open University.

Brennan, J. and Little, B. (1996) *A Review of Work-based Learning in Higher Education*. Sheffield: DfEE.

Brennan, J. and Jary, D. (2005) What is learned at university: The social and organisational mediation of university learning. SOMUL Working Paper No.1, York: HEA and OU/CHERI.

Davies, P. (1999). Rights and rites of passage: Crossing boundaries in France. *International Journal of Lifelong Education* 19(3): 215–224.

Department of Education and Science (DFES) (1987), *Meeting the Challenge*, Cm. 114. London: HMSO.

Department of Education and Science (DFES) (1991), *Higher Education – A New Framework*, Cm. 1541. London: HMSO.

Department for Education and Employment (DFEE) (1998). *The Learning Age*. London: HMSO.

Edwards, R. and Usher, R. (2000) *Globalisation and Pedagogy: Space, Place and Identity*. London: Routledge.

Enders, J., File, J., Huisman, J. and Westerheijden. D.F. (2005) *The European Higher Education and Research Landscape 2020: Scenarios and Strategic Debates*. Enschede: Center for Higher Education and Policy Studies (CHEPS), at http://www.utwente. nl/cheps/publications/downloadable_publications/downloadableenglish.doc/

European Commission (1995). *Teaching and Learning: Towards the Learning Society*. Luxembourg: Office for the Official Publications of the European Communities.

European Centre for the Development of Vocational Training (CEDEFOP) (2001) *Technology Will Improve Access to Learning for People with Disabilities*, at http://www2.trainingvillage.gr/etv/elearning/surveys/surmain.asp

Fieldhouse, R. (1996) *A History of Modern British Adult Education*. Leicester: NIACE.

Floud, R. (2001) Delivering the third mission – Does one size fit all? Presentation to Aim Higher: HERDA-SW Conference, 15–16 November 2001, at http://www.universitiesuk.ac.uk/speeches/show.asp?sp=44

Gallacher, J. (2005) Complementarity or differentiation: The roles of further education colleges and higher education institutions in Scotland's higher education system. In Gallacher, J. and Osborne, M. (eds) *A Contested Landscape: International Perspectives on Diversity in Mass Higher Education*. Leicester: National Institute for Adult and Continuing Education.

Gallacher, J., Osborne, M. and Postle, G. (1996) Increasing and widening access to higher education: A comparative study of policy and provision in Scotland and Australia. *International Journal of Lifelong Education* 15(6): 418–437.

Gellert, C. and Teichler, U. (1993) Introduction and chapter 1 in *Higher Education in Europe*. London: Jessica Kingsley.

Gooch, J. (1995). *Transplanting Extension: A New Look at the Wisconsin Idea*. Madison Wisconsin: UW-Extension Printing Services.

Harrison, R., Clarke, J., Reeve, F. and Edwards, R. (2003) Doing identity work: Fuzzy boundaries and flexibility in further education. *Research in Post-Compulsory Education* 8(1): 93–106.

HM Government (1995) *Competitiveness: Forging Ahead*, Cm. 2867. London: HMSO.

Lyotard, J.-F. (1984) *The Postmodern Condition: A Report on Knowledge*. Manchester: Manchester University Press.

McCarthy, C. (1912) *The Wisconsin Idea*. New York: McMillan Company, at http://www.library.wisc.edu/etext/WIReader/Contents/Idea.html

McDonald, A.S., Newton, P.E. and Whetton, C. (2001) *A Pilot of Aptitude Tests for University Entrance*. Slough: National Foundation for Educational Research for the Sutton Trust.

McGavock, K. and Osborne, M. (2005) Making a difference? A review of UK widening participation initiatives to medicine. *Journal of Access Policy and Practice* 3(1): 3–20.

McGivney, V. (1990) *Education's for other People: Access to Education for Non-participant Adults*. Leicester: National Institute for Adult and Continuing Education.

Morgan-Klein, B. (2003) Scottish higher education and the FE-HE nexus. *Higher Education Quarterly* 57(4): 338–354.

Morgan-Klein, B. and Murphy, M. (2002) Access and recruitment: Institutional policy in widening participation. In Trowler, P. (ed.) *Higher Education Policy and Institutional Change*. Buckingham: SRHE and Open University Press.

Murphy, M., Morgan-Klein, B., Osborne, M. and Gallacher, J. (2002) *Widening Participation in Higher Education: Report* to Scottish Executive. Stirling: Centre for Research in Lifelong Learning/Scottish Executive.

National Committee of Inquiry into Higher Education (NCIHE) (1997) *Higher Education in the Learning Society* (Dearing Report). London: National Committee of Inquiry into Higher Education.

Nicoll, K. (2006) *Flexibility & Lifelong Learning: Policy, Discourse, Politics*. London: Routledge.

Ortega, J. and Camara, E. (2001) Entry to university for adults over 25 years of age in Spain: Study of the current situation carried out by teachers and students of state centres of adult education. Proceedings of *Researching Widening Access: International Perspectives*. Glasgow: Centre for Research in Lifelong Learning.

Osborne, M. (2003a) A European comparative analysis of policy and practice in widening participation to lifelong learning. *European Journal of Education* 38(1): 5–24.

Osborne, M. (2003b) Policy and practice in widening participation – A six country comparative study. *International Journal of Lifelong Education* 22(1): 45–58.

Osborne, M. and Thomas, E. (Eds.) (2003) *Lifelong Learning in a Changing Continent: Continuing Education in the Universities of Europe*. Leicester: NIACE.

Osborne, M., Gallacher, J. and Crossan, B. (eds) (2004) *Researching Widening Access*. London: Routledge.

Osborne, M. (2005) Introduction. In Gallacher J. and Osborne, M. (eds) *A Contested Landscape: International Perspectives on Diversity in Mass Higher Education*. Leicester: National Institute for Adult and Continuing Education.

Pascarella, E.T. and Terenzini, P.T. (1991) *How College Affects Students. Findings and Insights from Twenty Years of Research*. San Francisco: Jossey-Bass.

Pascarella, E.T. and Terenzini, P.T. (2005) *How College Affects Students (Vol 2): A Third Decade of Research*. San Francisco: Jossey-Bass.

Percy, K., Ramsden, P. and Lewin, J. (1980) *Independent Study – Two Examples from English Higher Education*. Guildford: SRHE.

Schwartz, S. (2004) *Fair Admissions to Higher Education*. London: DfES.

Scott, P. (1995) *The Meaning of Mass Higher Education*. Buckingham: SRHE/OU.

Scottish Office Education and Industry Department (SOEID) (1998). *Opportunity Scotland: A Paper on Lifelong Learning*. Edinburgh: Stationery Office.

Scottish Higher Education Funding Council (SHEFC) (2000) *Wider Access Regional Forums*, Circular Letter FE56/2000. Edinburgh: Scottish Further Education Funding Council.

Teichler, U. (1998) *Changing Patterns of the HE System: The Experience of Three Decades*. London: Jessica Kingsley.

Thomas, L., May, H., Harrop, H., Houston, M., Knox, H., Lee, M.F., Osborne, M., Pudner, H. and Trotman, C. (2005) *From the Margins to the Mainstream*. London: UUK/SCOP.

Trow, M.A. (2005) Reflections on the transition from elite to mass to universal access: Forms and phases of higher education in modern societies since WWII. *Institute of Governmental Studies*. Working Paper, WP2005-4. Berkeley: University of California, accessible at http://repositories.cdlib.org/igs/WP2005-4.

Welsh Office (1998) *Learning is for Everyone*. Cardiff: Welsh Office.

Wheelahan, L. and Moodie, G. (2005) Separate post-compulsory education sectors within a liberal market economy: Interesting models generated by the Australian anomaly. In Gallacher, J. and Osborne, M. (eds) *A Contested Landscape: International Perspectives on Diversity in Mass Higher Education*. Leicester: National Institute for Adult and Continuing Education (NIACE).

Chapter 7

Learning at work

For a number of decades governments around the world have stressed the need for more effective training for both young people and adults and have linked this objective specifically to the needs of the labour market. There is a perceived need for a more highly trained and educated workforce to meet the requirements of the economy in the competitive, globalised and highly technological market of the early twenty-first century. Initial training and education are seen to be inadequate to meet the changing demands of the workplace and the workforce at all levels needs to access further education and training on a continuing basis in a world where lifetime employment in one career or job is no longer the norm. Commentators have used a variety of vivid expressions to describe the demands upon individuals and enterprises such as this: an era of *discontinuous change* (Handy, 1989) where the *half-life of knowledge* is decreasing (Barnett, 1994) and where to sustain economic advantage we have to work *smarter not harder* (Thurow, 1991). Given the changes in nature of work practices over the past few decades it might be more accurate for commentators with this perspective to say that all of us have to work 'smarter *and* harder'.

Since the 1980s, challenges of global competitiveness have been presented by governments in most Western nations as issues for both employers and educational institutions and this is reflected extensively in the process of policy making internationally (see Osborne, 2004 and Wolf, 2004). To quote the European Commission (2001, 6) '. . . competitive advantage is increasingly dependent on investment in human capital. Knowledge and competences are, therefore, also a powerful engine for economic growth. Given the current uncertain economic climate, investing in people becomes all the more important'.

This investment in human capital is now viewed as a lifelong process, and policies to encourage lifelong learning for work are of increasing importance across the globe. Four clear tendencies are observable in most societies:

1. For most of their history the offer of schools and universities has focused on the academic, and connections with the world of work have not been the concern of these institutions. Of course there have been notable exceptions,

but it is only in recent decades that attempts to make explicit curricular links with learning, employability and employment have been made.

2. Whereas traditionally resources have been front-loaded and provided to individuals in the main during the first two decades of their lives, considerably more concern is now placed on continuing education rather than simply initial education. Few areas of employment are immune from the requirement for Continuing Professional Development (CPD).

3. Furthermore, whilst provision has tended to be made available in prescribed spaces (normally formal educational institutions) and times (during daytime hours in the working week), in recent decades we observe more attention given to spatial and temporal flexibility of provision. This includes the provision of learning outside the boundaries of academy, including within the workplace.

4. Educational institutions have one clear market advantage: they offer accredited qualifications that are valued and valuable. Until recent times the awards could only be achieved by a small proportion of the (mainly young) population through highly prescribed mechanisms (e.g. a three- or four- year-residential period during which an institutionally determined route of study would be followed). Now, however, we see multiple means by which credit can be accumulated from a range of sources and transferred from one site of learning to another until the requisite points to obtain an award are achieved. Educational institutions still tend to maintain a hold on awarding powers, despite the emergence of corporate universities (e.g. the Motorola University) and new forms of accredited qualification (e.g. the European Computer Driving License (ECDL)). Increasingly, however, educational institutions are being induced to offer equivalence to demonstrable learning wherever it occurs including at the workplace. We see globally, and especially in Europe, on schemes generically termed as the *Recognition/Accreditation of Prior (Experiential) Learning* (R/AP(E)L).

We will consider each of these four trends in more detail, and they can be mapped onto a simple model (within which there is considerable complexity) of work-related learning. A useful overview of understandings of work-based learning is provided by Brennan and Little (1996) and in some of our previous research we defined three strands of work-based learning: learning for work, learning at work and learning through work (Seagraves *et al.*, 1996).

Learning for work is conceived as being broad and includes anything, which can be labelled "vocational". It can be delivered in school, colleges, universities, at home, from television, from the Internet or at work. *Learning at work* is related to training and development delivered inside organisations. It could be delivered by company personnel, consultants or staff from educational establishments. For both learning for and at work to be useful, there may need to be reinforcement by learning through work. *Learning through work* is integrated into the doing of a job; it includes the application of job-related learning and the skills and knowledge, which are acquired in the process of doing the job. These conceptions of workplace learning link to the work of a number of theorists in the fields of education and human resource development. These include the ideas of *reflection-in-action, single and double-loop learning* and *organisational learning* (Argyris and Schön, 1987, 1996), the *learning organisation* (Senge, 1990), *learning company* (Pedler, Burgoyne and Boydell, 1996), *critical reflection, experiential learning* (Dewey, 1938; Kolb and Fry, 1975 and Boud, Cohen and Walker, 1993), *self-directed learning* (Candy, 1991), *independent learning* (Brookfield, 1990) and *work-process knowledge* (Boreham, Fischer and Samurçay, 2002; Boreham, 2004).

Connecting the academy to work (learning for work)

In an earlier chapter we considered the role of schools in lifelong learning. One debate within school education concerns the extent to which it is possible or indeed desirable to explicitly include within the curriculum studies, which specifically seek to prepare young people for working life. A number of schemes labelled variously 'Skills for Work', 'Entrepreneurship Education', 'Enterprise Education' and suchlike have been incorporated into school curricula. The following quote from work being undertaken in the European Union[1] is typical of attempts in many societies to embed this perspective into early 'learning for life'.

> According to surveys, 60% of EU citizens have never considered setting up a business. "These figures reflect an attitude that needs to be changed to achieve the Lisbon objectives in terms of growth and employment", said Commissioner Figel, in charge of education, training, culture, and multi-lingualism. Speaking at the first 'Entrepreneurship in Education European Summit', organised by JA-YE Europe, he stressed: "We need to make our societies and citizens think positively about starting new businesses." According to JA-YE, a provider of enterprise education programmes, entrepreneurship education plays an essential role in shaping attitudes, skills and culture. The earlier and more widespread the exposure to entrepreneurship and innovation, the more likely it is that students will consider becoming entrepreneurs. The commissioner said it is crucial to support the take-up of entrepreneurship programmes, from primary school to university, focusing in particular on secondary schools, where spreading the message: "You can create your own job", by involving students in mini-companies for instance, can quadruple the chances of young people creating their own company.
>
> (EurActive.com, 2006)

Similarly in Higher Education (HE) systems throughout the world, there has been debate about the preparedness of graduates for the world of work. In the US, for example, some commentators considered that the malaise had set in as early as the 1960s (see Gaff, 1983), and that it reflected the decline in the general education of undergraduates. Gaff reports on a number of HE initiatives in the US that sought to combat this perceived deficiency of the system. At a time we should recall that lifelong learning was still an embryonic concept in most of the world, but he notes that in most projects it was 'a requirement that it (the curriculum) include the mastery of the linguistic, analytic, critical and computational skills necessary for life-long learning'. Three specific projects in the 1980s are of particular note and were major contributors to the development of the concept of the *generic/transferable skill* which emerged as an element of general education objectives in HE. These were the *General Educational Models* (GEM) project, the *College Outcomes Measures Project* (COMP) and the American Programme Evaluation Project (APEP). Gradually more detailed lists of generic skills have emerged, their emphases being both on those skills required to operate efficiently in society and on those that respond specifically to employer requirements. For example, the American Society for Training and Development (ASTD) and the U.S. Department of Labor identified 16 skills collapsed into a hierarchy of seven groups called the Workplace Basics, described as those skills that employers want. These are as follows: learning to learn, reading, writing and computation; listening and oral communication; creative thinking and problem solving; self-esteem; goal setting/motivation, personal and career development; interpersonal skills/negotiation and teamwork; and organisational effectiveness and leadership (Carnevale, Gainer and Meltzer, 1990).

Many such models have been developed throughout the world (e.g. Mayer, 1992 in Australia), the underlying assumptions being that discipline-specific knowledge and skills is not enough. Of course to become a pharmacist, dental technician, translator or a raft of other specialists is unlikely without specialist knowledge, but that may not be enough to perform well and advance in a job. In the case of many other jobs, it is not the discipline specificity of the qualification that is important, but rather measures of what an individual has learned in a generic sense. As a consequence, most institutions of post-compulsory education will now include explicit programmes of study within their curriculum that provide students with opportunities to demonstrate the possession of these generic skills. These may take the form of the integration within all disciplines of learning outcomes described as being *generic* or *transferable skills*. Alternatively, there may be discrete and often credit-bearing programmes that more explicitly focus on the connection between academia and work in topics such as career planning and entrepreneurship. Internships in business, commerce and in the public sector seek to make similar connections, and many texts are devoted to making the implicit explicit (see, for example, Hettich and Helkowski, 2004). However, there have been many criticisms of the notion that generic skills can be taught or learnt independent of a context and applied readily in new contexts (Perkins and Salomon, 1989; Billett, 2000 – see also Winterton, Le Deist and Stringfellow, 2005 for a comprehensive overview).

It also could be that all this is irrelevant if we take the view that a qualification is simply what Spence (1973) describes as a *signalling* device, and points to capabilities that are only loosely associated with its core knowledge content or skills base. At its extreme, as Wolf (2004, 318) suggests, signalling models would argue that the higher pay of the more highly educated has 'nothing to do with academic or vocational skills learned in education', but is a function of the supposed association of schooling with 'innate ability, or its association with psychological and personality traits such as diligence'. The idea of 'innate ability' is, to say the least, controversial. However, we could substitute here the links between cultural capital, class and education. As we argued in Chapter 2, dispositional cultural capital is often read as 'natural ability' because the process of acquiring it is largely hidden from view. It is clearly an important 'signalling' device. Moreover, institutional cultural capital in the form of what kind of school or university is attended is also likely to be relevant. There is good evidence that it is the label of the institution that provides the main strength within the signal. In the UK (in)famously there now appear advertisements for good graduates from 'older' institutions. Furthermore, prospects of attending such institutions, especially those which are most selective, are, as we point out in Chapter 6, to a certain extent a function of early schooling, socio-economic class and parental wealth.

Continuing professional development (learning at work)

As we argue in Chapter 4, there is little doubt that an investment in education creates an economic benefit at an individual level. Simple correlations of years of schooling with lifetime earnings show a positive relation, and although similar calculations with respect to lifelong learning are less common, a similar trend is discernable, albeit with significant caveats (OECD, 2001).

Furthermore, most individuals consider that economic and career enhancement is the principle benefit of learning at work, and view the workplace as the principal likely location of continuing learning. As Billet (2001) says, 'For many workers, perhaps most, the workplace represents the only or most viable location to initially learn and or/develop their vocational practice'. However, two clear points can be made about individuals' reasons for engagement in work-related learning.

First, as we also point out in Chapter 4, at an individual level direct economic reward is not the sole reason for individuals undertaking programmes of learning, and these include learning within the workplace. There are a number of other personal benefits to engagement in workplace learning, a number of which are congruent with the perspectives of enterprises. For businesses, arguments in favour of offering educational opportunities to employees have been assessed by many researchers. For example, the benefits of Employee Development Programmes such as Ford EDAP have been assessed in the UK by Parsons, Cocks and Rowe (1998). Such initiatives have been developed by a number of companies to provide non-job related learning opportunities in collaboration with trade unions. Benefits are reported to include encouraging a *learning culture*, contributing to the improvement of productivity, efficiency and customer service and enhancing the confidence, morale, commitment and motivation of the workforce. An alternative view is that such schemes largely benefit the company in one way – they are cheaper to fund than pay rises.

Second, economic benefits may not necessarily be sufficient in themselves. An apt example in this context is the incentives to teachers to engage in structured continuing professional development in Scotland. The economic arguments are inescapable with benefits over a lifetime estimated to be as much as £200,000 for some individuals given that salary rises will be also reflected in improved pensions. Yet, despite the availability of interest-free loans to take qualifications, take-up has been poor. According to a recent report, in 2004–2005, only half of the money needed to fund expected pay rises for teachers progressing to chartered status was required (HM Inspectorate of Education (HMIE) 2007, 8). The evidence suggests that economic gain in at least some teachers' thinking is balanced against the upfront financial costs and time required. Nonetheless, since economic benefit is clearly a principal concern of individuals and companies, this factor deserves further attention. As we have previously suggested the link between level of qualification and getting a job, keeping a job or getting promotion and salary rises has historically been clear. Furthermore, undertaking learning whilst in work is a highly rational decision to make since this reduces losses in income and in benefits (such as pension contributions). By contrast, taking time out of work to learn, especially in the later years of life, can have a negative impact on lifetime earnings (OECD, 2001). This raises issues not only of the places where learning can be accessed, but also modes of delivery and times when opportunities are available, all of which are considered later.

Most companies, however, despite the merits of the variety of outcomes of investing in the learning of their employees look to the 'bottom line'. Is there evidence that this investment will lead to increased profitability? Here the evidence is less clear, and becomes less convincing especially when we consider small to medium-sized enterprises (SMEs). It is difficult to demonstrate that investment in lifelong learning by companies is a direct factor in increasing profits since there are so many factors that play a role, most notably prevailing economic markets, competition and adequate capitalisation. The argument concerning education and financial returns is similar to that which pertains to educational achievement and the economic productivity of a nation a whole. We have previously quoted Wolf (2004) in the context of the simple proxies that economists use. If investing in education increases productivity, so how could companies fail to see the logic of providing lifelong learning by the bucketful? And although Wolf's arguments are not specific to workplace learning, her assertions that higher earnings of individuals are not simply a function of education and training, and that higher wages equals higher productivity is not as strong as economists suggest, would no doubt cause companies to be cautious. Furthermore, from a purely rational economic perspective, investing in current human capital might be a poorer investment by comparison to investing in staff who are already trained and often cheaper. Although ethically questionable, it might be more economically efficient for OECD countries to import well-trained specialists from Central and Eastern Europe or Africa than upskill their own populations. This tendency has been observed in areas such as nursing and might also apply in the future in technical areas given the lack of supply of home-trained workers in some fields. Since the accession of new countries from Central and Eastern Europe to the European Union there has been significant migration to the West. Journalists such as Asthana (2005) report that the 'Polish plumber' represents all that is controversial about the European constitution, and are the focus of considerable xenophobia in the UK. However, Poles like many other nationalities often simply are filling a skills gap.

The extent to which the possible merits of work-based programmes might be recognised at corporate and individual level within SMEs is certainly open to question. Although they play a vital role in the development of the economy-stimulating competition, developing new technologies and new products and creating new jobs, such organisations frequently do not have the human resource development expertise and infrastructure which larger companies enjoy. It is less likely that their employees can take advantage of personal and professional development opportunities through in-company provision and/or access to further and higher education. These problems are often seen to be compounded by lack of financial resources, higher labour mobility, tight schedules with no 'slack' to allow employees time away from the workplace and insufficient numbers of employees needing training at any one time to provide it in-house. Furthermore, research evidence suggests that the economic benefit to SMEs in investing in employees is not demonstrated (Storey and Westhead, 1994). Nonetheless, there is evidence that companies will invest in their staff when driven by external constraints that require organisational change, introduction of new technology or compliance with legislation (Billet and Smith, 2003); Shipley (2001) adds other factors that might motivate employers including performance management, strategic planning, succession planning, industrial relations and innovation.

Learning spaces and places

The notion of learning at work links to the notions of flexibility introduced in the previous chapter and in particular to learning in spaces and places that would not have been conceived of in quite the same way by previous generations. Whilst learning at work has existed historically within the tradition of pre-vocational training in the form of apprenticeships and their modern equivalents, these schemes have tended to be bounded within very tight structures. The UK Modern Apprenticeship scheme, for example, provides opportunities for those aged 16 and over to obtain awards within the Vocational Qualifications (VQ) structure whilst in employment (DfES, 2004). Once restricted to those aged 25 and under, since 2004, there have also been Adult Apprenticeships in the UK aimed to address skills shortages and encourage career change. Although now potentially a target for reform (Deissinger and Hellwig, 2005), famously Germany has a long tradition of offering apprenticeships within the Duales System combining work in an enterprise with theoretical learning in a vocational school. Many other countries have a history of apprenticeship schemes, but these models are but one form of learning at work.

Contemporary flexibility in the context of workplace learning generally relates to arrangement whereby existing workers can access learning in locations and modes, and at times that to at least to a certain degree are of their choosing rather than of institutions. It also involves challenges to the nature and acquisition of knowledge, and new ways for recognition/accreditation of prior (experiential) learning (R/AP(E)L) that we introduced previously, and which are detailed below. It also may depend on significant structural modification in systems of education, that allow accredited learning to be 'banked' and translated into qualifications, namely qualification frameworks. At its simplest, learning at work may simply be the offering of a traditional qualification in a workplace or offering initial or continuing training to do a job. Many organisations make arrangements with providers of education and training that allows provision to be delivered at workplaces with varying degrees of flexibility in terms of timing and mode. Other employers deliver training themselves, and in the case of some larger organisations through what are described as 'corporate universities'.[2] There are, however, a number of nuanced aspects to the workplace as an arena for learning as illustrated by learning *through* work.

Learning through work and its accreditation

Learning through work has also been conceptualised in the context of organi-sational change, and a case study by Boreham (2004) is particularly helpful. He uses the term *work process knowledge* when referring to the knowledge needed for working in flexible and innovative business environments. These include those environments in which ICTs are utilised to integrate production functions that previously have been separated. He argues that in such work contexts, a systems-level understanding of the work process of organisation as a whole is required in order that employees may understand their interconnectedness with other parts of the system. Work process knowledge is described by Boreham as *'active' knowledge*, and is that used directly in the performance of work. More often than not this knowledge is constructed by employees when they are solving problems in the workplace, and involves a fusion of 'know-how' with abstract theory. In a case study of a vocational curriculum currently being adopted by a German automotive manufacture, he describes key curricular features, namely 'using a model of the work process as the curriculum framework, co-producing (and co-delivering) the curriculum using integrated teams of staff from the vocational school and the workplace, and fusing the different knowledge resources of the vocational school and the workplace into a single activity system'.

It is important to distinguish between the learning that occurs through the process of work, and the value that is ascribed to it. Much learning occurs through doing a job that is neither measured nor desirable of measurement, but much of the emphasis within lifelong learning policy statements has been on the accreditation of prior experiential learning especially in the workplace. We have discussed the work-process knowledge model above, which at an organisational level provides a framework that can be put into place to develop the knowledge and skills of individuals and thereby may contribute to capacity building within enterprises. Additionally, a focus on learning through work can build upon the strong evidence base of the perceived desire by individuals for work-related learning opportunities. However, in order for such learning to assume a currency, new and flexible forms of accreditation of learning may be desirable.

The accreditation of learning at and through work

Accreditation of Prior Experiential Learning (APEL) is not exclusively tied to the workplace, but that environment presents considerable potential for procedures for the accreditation of learning, and is one focus of the activity of a number of organisations in the field, including the well-established Council for the Accreditation of Experiential Learning (CAEL) in the US and the learning from Experience Trust (LET)[3] in the UK. APEL can trace its theoretical precepts back to the work of John Dewey (1938) in experiential learning, and is heavily influenced by Kolb's Experiential Learning Cycle (Kolb and Fry, 1975). Its main precepts are that learning which occurs outside of formal institutions *is* potentially measurable and accreditable against formal qualifications, that it is the demonstration of learning that is more important than the process by which that learning took place, and that individuals should not have to spend their time and money in following traditional courses if they can demonstrate *competence* already. We encounter here another ostensibly simple word, but it should be noted that it is subject to a number of interpretations.[4] In a minimalist sense, competence is tied closely to performance of individuals at work and tends to be linked to the specified standards of occupations as in VQ systems such as those in the UK, Australia and New Zealand.

For some commentators APEL represents a radical challenge to current educational practices. For example, Feutrie (2000) see the French system of *La Validation des Acquis de l'Experience* (VAE), as one which represents a challenge to the nature and locus of knowledge; and a challenge to institutions to recognise the diversity of people's opportunities for learning. As a consequence, VAE becomes part of the armoury of widening participation in as much as that it is one means of combating the discriminatory effects of social and economic division. Ultimately, it is argued, VAE presents fundamental challenges to the structure of traditional higher education qualifications such the French *diplôme* (Davies, 1999).

Elsewhere (Murphy *et al.*, 2002) we have previously described how systems of APEL can be conceptualised as lying within the panapoly of access initiatives to higher education. Not only are such systems about the accumulation of credit to achieve an award, but they also represent a particular form of flexibility by which entry to institutions might be achieved. For example, by constructing a portfolio of evidence of learning equivalent to that which would secure entry to an undergraduate degree through traditional qualifications gained at school, an adult might be able to gain entry to higher education. And there is good evidence of demand in some societies. For example, in Canada according to a 2004 national survey of over 9,000 adults within the Work and Lifelong Learning (WALL)[5] project demonstrated that over a half would consider enrolling in learning programmes if prior learning assessment were available. Livingstone and Myers (2007) argue that this in Canada alone translates, when scaled-up, to an unmet demand from 12 million people who might like their informal learning achievements to be assessed and potentially accredited towards qualifications. However effective and efficient procedures might be, optimism in the openness of systems to radical practices does not always bear fruit. Rhetoric can outshine practice. In France, Feutrie and Gallacher (2003) report that schemes of VAE have largely failed in their assault on traditional educational structures, and there have been many disappointments in the success of work-based schemes with a notable lack of commitment from companies.

France nonetheless presents perhaps the most comprehensive of national models. In other societies, however, we find even greater expectations. For example, in South Africa, the recognition/accreditation of prior (experiential) learning (R/AP(E)L) has been described as having a potential role in radical social transformation (Michelson, 1997). In the UK, everyone concerned with continuing education and widening participation will have heard of APEL, but in practice most will not have awarded credit or implemented access using the tools it offers. The common mantra is that the process is burdensome to institutions, costs too much, is simply about credentialism and is not a process of learning. This may be as much about defending boundaries as it is a legitimate criticism of APEL procedures. Whilst schemes of APEL do tend to emphasise outcome over process there is good evidence, for example, from work in both Canada and France that the process in itself may for some individuals be an empowering one. Moreover, as Livingstone and Myers (2007) suggest, it may have significant spin-offs not only in participation in formal learning, but also in 'labour market participation, workplace productivity, career advancement, voluntary engagement and community development'.

Furthermore having credentials may be necessary, although as we saw earlier these are not always a sufficient pre-requirement to compete in the certain sectors of employment. On the other hand, it should be recognised that in a changing economy, the nature of work opportunity is changing too. Keep and Mayhew (2004) report a number of studies that many service level jobs in hotels, stores, bars and restaurants place less weight on qualifications than on uncertified skills, personal characteristics and attributes.

Concluding remarks

Policies with regard to lifelong learning tend to encompass a tripartite relationship of the individual, enterprises and the state. In such models the individual is increasingly given the responsibility for ensuring their own employability. Governments may contribute to this process through the co-financing of schemes such as the UK's Independent Learning Account (ILA) programme, which has been replicated elsewhere,[6] but ultimately in most societies it is the individual and/or employers who are expected to be the major contributors.

Learning at, through and for work are all important features of workplace learning and involve varying degrees of challenge to current practices for all stakeholders. For educational institutions, there is a challenge to the locus of control of knowledge since a key assumption underpinning workplace learning is that much valuable learning occurs outwith the boundaries of HEIs and other post-compulsory institutions and therefore beyond their control. The reduction of the role of an educational institution to that of a recognition or accrediting agency typically evokes the response that they are becoming nothing more than 'degree-mills'. This is of course an extreme position, but it exists, and does raise fundamental questions of epistemology and institutional position. In a competitive market, being a partner in workplace learning may be a necessary flexible institutional response for some institutions within a mixed economy of provision, and more positively a legitimate response to new 'consumer demands'. At the employer end, as we have pointed out, whilst they do not always obviously see the benefits of investing in employees, advantages do exist. Potentially, all players win if an individual can combine work-related study with employment. Of course, there are caveats about accumulating credit without clearly planned development and progression, and it might be argued that such mechanisms are no more than credentialism. We would add two further qualifications. First, as we note in Chapter 8, the relevance of certification in the learning society may be overplayed since some research indicates that many individuals learn informally on the job. Second, as we note in Chapter 3, across OECD countries, employers have been relatively reluctant to invest in training at all, and when they do, they are most likely to invest in the most qualified and highly paid workers. Learning at work, then, would seem to offer no escape from the familiar problem of inequality of access.

Recognition and accreditation of learning that has occurred within workplace environments, though rather overemphasising outcomes over learning processes by the advocates of R/AP(E)L, can be an important potential component of the lifelong learning offer. It potentially gives value to otherwise unacknowledged learning, and hence further opportunity for progression, especially in workplaces, to individuals who would otherwise might not be able to do so. However, it is a product derived from learning, a fact often ignored by the advocates of the process.

Notes

1 See http://ec.europa.eu/enterprise/enterprise_policy/index_en.htm for further details of the European Commission's Enterprise policy.
2 See, for example, McDonald's Hamburger University (http://www.mcdonalds.com/corp/career/hamburger_university.html) and Motorola University (http://www.motorola.com/content.jsp?globalObjectId=3084).For more details see Allen (2002).
3 For more details of CAEL, see http://www.cael.org/and for LET see http://www.learningexperience.org.uk/index.php.
4 Feetrie (1998) presents four interpretations of competence, pointing out for example that the individualism of VQ approaches ignores the complexity of many workplaces where individual performance is indistinguishable from that of the group, and this has led to discussions in the French system of *collective savoir-faire* (collective competence). Students in HE may be reminded of the difficulties of negotiating collective assessment since measures of performance are inexorably individual. See also Pouget and Osborne (2004) for a discussion of French and UK systems of VAP/APEL.
5 Voices of some of these learners can be found in DVD clips at http://www.wallnetwork.ca and http://www.placentre.ns.ca.
6 See, for example, Renkema (2006) for an account of Dutch experiences and calls for Personal Competitiveness Accounts in the US (National Center for Education and the Economy, 2007).

References

Allen, M. (2002) (ed.) *The Corporate University Handbook: Designing, Managing, and Growing a Successful Program.* New York: AMACOM/American Management Association.

Argyris, C. and Schön, D.A. (1987) *Theory and Practice: Increasing Professional Effectiveness.* San Francisco: Jossey Bass.

Argyris, C. and Schön, D.A. (1996) *Organisational Learning II: Theory, Method and Practice.* Reading, Mass: Addison Wesley.

Asthana, A. (2005) The Polish plumber who fixed the vote. *Observer,* 29 May 2005.

Barnett, R. (1994). *The Limits of Competence: Knowledge, Higher Education and Society.* Buckingham: Society for Research into Higher Education and Open University Press.

Billett, S. (2000). Performance at work: Identifying smart work practice. In Gerber, R. and Lankshear, C. (eds) *Training for a Smart Workforce.* London: Routledge, pp. 123–150.

Billett, S. (2001) Participation and continuity at work: A critique of current workplace learning discourses. Context, power and perspective: Confronting the challenges to improving attainment in learning at work. *Joint Network/SKOPE/TRLP International Workshop,* 8–10 November 2001, Sunley Management Centre, University College of Northampton, accessible at http://www.infed.org/archives/e-texts/billett_workplace_learning

Billet, S. and Smith, A. (2003) Compliance, engagement and commitment: Increasing employer expenditure in training. *Journal of Vocational Education and Training* 55(3): 281–299.

Boreham, N. (2004) Orienting the work-based curriculum towards work process knowledge: A rationale and a German case study. *Studies in Continuing Education* 26(2): 209–227.

Boreham, N., Fischer, M. and Samurçay, R. (2002) *Work Process Knowledge.* New York: Routledge.

Boud, D., Cohen, R. and Walker, D. (eds) (1993) *Using Experience for Learning*. Buckingham: Oxford University Press.

Brennan, J. and Little, B. (1996) *A Review of Work-based Learning in Higher Education*. Sheffield: DfEE.

Brookfield, S. (1990) *The Skilful Teacher: On Technique, Trust and Responsiveness*. San Francisco: Jossey Bass.

Candy, P.C. (1991) *Self-direction for Lifelong Learning: A Comprehensive Guide to Theory and Practice*. San Francisco: Jossey Bass.

Carnevale, A.P., Gainer, L.J. and Meltzer, A.S. (1990) *Workplace Basics: The Essential Skills Employers Want*. San Francisco: Jossey-Bass.

Davies, P. (1999) Rights and rites of passage: Crossing boundaries in France. *International Journal of Lifelong Education* 19(3): 215–224.

Deissinger, T. and Hellwig, S. (2005) Apprenticeships in Germany: Modernising the dual system. *Education and Training* 47 (4–5): 312–324.

Department for Education and Skills (DfES) (2004) *21st Century Apprenticeships – End to End Review of the Delivery of Modern Apprenticeships*. London: DfES/LSC.

Dewey, J. (1938) *Experience and Education*. London: Collier MacMillan Publishers.

EurActive.com (2006) *EU Education Systems not Producing Enough Entrepreneurs*, at http://www.euractiv.com/en/innovation/eu-education-systems-producing-entrepreneurs/article-157666

European Commission (2001) *Making the Lifelong Learning Area a Reality*. Brussels: EC.

Feutrie, M. (2000) France: The story of La Validation des Acquis [Recognition of experiential learning]. In N. Evans (ed.) *Experiential Learning around the World. Employability and the Global Economy*. London: Jessica Kingsley Publishers, p. 108.

Feutrie, M. and Gallacher, J. (2003) Recognising and accrediting informal and non-formal learning within higher education: An analysis of the issues emerging from a study of France and Scotland. *European Journal of Education* 38(1): 71–83.

Gaff, J.G. (1983). *General Education Today: A Critical Analysis of Controversies, Practices and Reforms*. San Francisco: Jossey Bass.

Handy, C. (1989) *The Age of Unreason*. London: Hutchison.

HM Inspectorate of Education (HMIE) (2007) *Teaching Scotland's Children*. Edinburgh: HMIE.

Hettich, P. and Helkowski, C. (2004) *Connecting College to Career: Student Guide to Work and Life Transition*. Belmont: Wadsworth.

Keep, E. and Mayhew, K. (2004) The economic and distributional implications of current roles on higher education. Oxford Review of Economic Policy 20(2): 298–314.

Kolb, D. and Fry, R. (1975) Towards an applied theory of experiential learning. In C. Cooper (ed.) *Theories of Group Practices*. London: Wiley.

Livingstone, D. and Myers, D. (2007) 'I might be overqualified': Personal perspectives and national survey findings on prior learning assessment and recognition in Canada. *Journal of Adult and Continuing Education*. 13(1).

Mayer, E. (1992) Employment-related key competencies for post-compulsory education and training. Discussion Paper. Melbourne: Ministry of Education and Training.

Michelson, E. (1997) The politics of memory: The recognition of experiential learning. In Walters, S. (ed.) *Globalization, Adult Education & Training: Impacts and Issues*. London: Zed Books, p. 145.

Murphy, M., Morgan-Klein, B., Osborne, M. and Gallacher, J. (2002) *Widening Participation in Higher Education: Report* to *Scottish Executive*. Stirling: Centre for Research in Lifelong Learning/Scottish Executive.

National Center for Education and the Economy (NCEE) (2007) *Tough Choices or Tough Times – Report of the National Commission on the Skills of the American Workforce*. Washington DC: National Center for Education and the Economy.

Organisation for Economic Co-operation and Development (OECD) (2001) *Economics and Finance of Lifelong Learning*. Paris: OECD.

Osborne, M. (2004) Work process knowledge and lifelong learning policies. In Fischer, M., Boreham, N. and B. Nyham, B. (eds) *European Perspectives on Learning at Work. The Acquisition of Work Process Knowledge*, CEDEFOP Reference Series 56. Luxembourg: Office for Official Publications of the European Communities.

Parsons, D., Cocks, N. and Rowe, V. (1998) *The Role of the Employee Development Schemes in Increasing Learning at Work*. DfEE Research Report 73. Sudbury: DfEE.

Pedler, M., Burgoyne, J. and Boydell, T. (1996) *The Learning Company. A strategy for Sustainable Development*. London: McGraw-Hill.

Perkins, D.N. and Salomon, G. (1989) Are cognitive skills context bound? *Educational Researcher*, 18(1): 16–25.

Pouget, M. and Osborne, M. (2004) Accreditation or validation of prior experiential learning: Knowledge and *saviors* in France – A different perspective. *Studies in Continuing Education* 26(1): 45–65.

Renkema, A. G. (2006) *Individual Learning Accounts: A Strategy for Lifelong Learning?* 's-Hertogenbosch: Cinop

Seagraves, L., Osborne, M.J., Dockrell, R., Neal, P., Hartshorn, C. and Boyd, A. (1996). *LISC Final Report*. Stirling: University of Stirling/Employment Department.

Senge, P.M. (1990) *The Fifth Discipline. The Art and Practice of the Learning Organization*. London: Random House.

Shipley, N. (2001) Smart work: What industry needs from partnership. In Boud, D. and Solomon, N. (eds) *Work-based Learning: A New Higher Education?* Buckingham: Open University Press, pp. 141–154.

Spence, A.M. (1973) Job market signalling. *Quarterly Review of Economics*, 2(3): 355–374.

Storey, D. and Westhead, P. (1994) *Management Training and Small Firm Performance: A Critical Review*. Working Paper 18. Warwick: Warwick Business School, University of Warwick

Thurow, L.C. (1991). Americans have to work smarter, not harder. *McCall's*, April, pp. 32-33

Winterton, J., Delamare-Le Deist, F. and Stringfellow, E. (2005) *Typology of Knowledge, Skills and Competences: Clarification of the Concept and Prototype*. Toulouse: Centre for European Research on Employment and Human Resources, Groupe ESC Toulouse, at http://www.ecotec.com/europeaninventory/publications/method/CEDEFOP_typology.pdf

Wolf, A. (2004) Education and economic performance: Simplistic theories and their policy consequences. *Oxford Review of Economic Policy*, 20(2): 315–333.

Chapter 8

Learning in the community and home

> If all learning were to be represented by an iceberg, then the section above the surface of the water would be sufficient to cover formal learning, but the submerged two thirds of the structure would be needed to convey the much greater importance of informal learning.
>
> (Coffield, 2000, 1)

In this chapter we discuss the importance of non-formal or informal[1] learning in the community and in the family and the implications of lifelong learning policies for such learning. As the Coffield quotation makes clear, it is difficult to overestimate the importance of informal learning; not just in the 'accidental' learning we do as we negotiate our relationships and personal lives, but also in learning for and at work. For example, in a survey of adults in a South Wales mining community, Fevre, Gorard and Rees (2000) found that despite the growth of formal training in the workplace, many individuals said that they had taught themselves to do their jobs. For these individuals, any formal training that they participated in occurred after they had already 'learned' the job and that for this reason, formal training was often undertaken to achieve a 'paper qualification' for a job that they already understood. Fevre, Gorard and Rees conclude that this suggests that the 'learning society' places too much emphasis on certification. Lifelong learning policies of the 1990s have certainly been criticised for having concentrated mainly on participation and learning in educational institutions and on formal qualifications. The primary criticism here, then, is that lifelong learning policies and practices underestimate the importance of informal learning in their focus on getting more people to participate in learning in formal settings.

In the UK these criticisms were fuelled by the formalisation of some types of 'informal' adult education in the mid-1990s and the growing significance of NQFs in defining learning content and outcomes (Osborne, 2003). Increasingly, learning which is not tied to formal qualifications as defined by national frameworks has failed to attract funding, so that even relatively informal community learning is to be attached to NQFs (see Scottish Executive, 2004 for such an example). Thus one impact of lifelong learning policies has been to formalise learning. This implies greater regulation of course, but it is also possible that it may open up educational pathways, making the achievement of certification possible for the most socially excluded learners. More recently, social policies aimed at building individual and community capacity in the UK reveal a renewed interest in learning in informal settings such as local communities. These policies focus on the social benefits of learning, which may be realised in learning that does not lead to formal qualifications. One example of this is education for parenthood which takes place in a variety of local settings. Some might argue that such provision does not qualify as 'informal', however, particularly if it is provided by the state rather than created by local communities. This chapter considers the relevance of informal learning to the development of a 'learning society' including an evaluation of learning in the community and in the family. However, we begin by considering the meaning of 'informal' learning.

What is informal learning?

Definitions of informal learning differ widely between commentators. Some prefer the definition of non-formal learning or non-formal education. Colley, Hodkinson and Malcolm (2003) provide a useful overview of theories and definitions, identifying four different terms in use, namely *non-formal education, informal education, non-formal learning* and *informal learning*. The distinctions made between these depend on which aspects are being highlighted. While some writers attempt to distinguish between different types of learning processes or differences in epistemology, others are concerned with the political dimensions (particularly the purpose) of different types of learning. The term *non-formal education* has, for example, often been used to describe practices that are oppositional to mainstream provision.[2] These practices and definitions are inevitably historically specific and Colley, Hodkinson and Malcolm trace the genealogy of the concept, locating it in five 'historical moments'. Their discussion demonstrates that the meanings we attach to informal (or non-formal) learning inevitably change over time. Colley, Hodkinson and Malcolm observe, for example, that in adult education practice, non-formal education has been and is assigned a positive value as accessible, alternative and even oppositional to mainstream provision. In contemporary theoretical formulations, some writers such as Eraut prefer the term *non-formal* to informal since *informal* has connotations of casualness while others such as the European Commission make a clear distinction between informal and non-formal learning[3] (Colley, Hodkinson and Malcolm, 2003).

For the purpose of this discussion, we have used the term *informal learning* to denote learning that either takes place outside of institutions or is defined by some other element of 'informality' such as non-certified learning. This is a wide definition, one which encapsulates both intentional and unintentional learning. We have also chosen to use *learning*, rather than education because it implies greater fluidity for example as in accidental learning which takes place even where there is no provision formal or otherwise. This naturally embraces a very great deal of learning types indeed – for example, learning to bath a baby, or how to obtain a swift divorce, as well as more clearly defined learning episodes such as learning how to use a computer at home. Moreover, this definition may also include certain types of learning in the workplace, much of which is informal in nature (Fevre, Gorard and Rees, 2000). As we have already noted, in adult education practice, informal learning is often assigned a positive value. It is sometimes associated with a humanistic purpose such as 'learning for its own sake' as opposed to the utilitarian purpose that is often associated with formal learning. Therefore some definitions of informal learning contain assumptions about the *value* of that kind of learning as opposed to 'formal' learning. By implication, or explicitly, formal learning is characterised as 'teacher focused' rather than 'learner focused'; thus inferring that learners will have little influence over the content or the processes of learning. In addition, it is often argued that formal learning is relatively inaccessible to certain kinds of learners and/or inappropriate, in situations where individuals and communities may want to define their own agendas. Debates about the nature and value of informal learning have therefore often been polarised with a focus on the *differences* between formal and informal learning rather than on their *similarities*. Along with concerns about the purpose of the learning, the commitment to the idea that informal learning is in some ways more desirable than formal learning is often associated with particular learning theories, such as social learning models[4] which tend to emphasise informal learning processes. Apart from the question of debates over value, there are two further problems in defining what we understand by informal learning.

First, it is difficult to draw a clear boundary between informal and formal learning – even when using definitions more refined than our rather general one. To return to our earlier example of informal learning, many prospective parents in the UK will learn how to bath their baby in prenatal classes, which may take place in a variety of settings either formal or informal. In many instances, though not all, these classes will be provided free by the state and be delivered by trained midwives or health visitors, who may have had limited formal training in teaching and learning – or even none at all. The content is likely to be partly predetermined and to include some formal information such as the timing of compulsory assessments of infants and societal expectations of the participants as parents. The learning processes themselves will almost certainly contain both formal and informal aspects. The classes are unlikely to be compulsory for most parents, although teaching and learning approaches will probably vary. Therefore, learning to bath a baby in contemporary society contains elements of formal *and* informal learning and as a consequence, is difficult to assign to either category. Notably, as this example of a learning process illustrates, it contains utilitarian, even regulatory, elements as well as humanistic and voluntaristic elements. Second, since learning is socially embedded, the way we think about learning and the significance that we attach to it changes over time. As we have already stated, in adult education practice, informal learning has been variously associated with 'alternative' or 'emancipatory' educational practices. These have been associated with social movements in the UK in the last two centuries and political or popular education in post-colonial countries in the second half of the twentieth century.[5] We also find elements of informal learning defined as 'alternative' or 'oppositional' in social reformist education and welfare-state initiatives, particularly in deprived communities in the twentieth century, but also in current initiatives in community learning. In the current climate of lifelong learning policy, informal learning is often associated with growing governmental interest in the social benefits of learning and the capacities of individuals and communities to make changes. In this context, informal learning is increasingly related to discussions of the importance of social capital for learning (Baron, Wilson and Riddell, 2000; see also Field and Spence, 2000).[6]

The meanings and social significance of informal learning vary according to social context as the widely differing practices of informal learning demonstrate. The social and political significance of these strands are a matter for debate. We return to the contemporary emphasis on community learning below. What is important to note here is that the concept of informal learning is often linked with various political aims. In summary, then, the meaning of informal learning is relatively fluid. It is historically specific and changes over time. In adult education theory and practice, it has had a clear political dimension and the debate over definitions of informal and formal learning has often been polarised. However, many learning 'episodes' contain both informal and formal elements. Nevertheless, informal learning has been assigned a particular and positive value in adult education. We can expect lifelong learning policies and practices to impact upon informal learning. Policies in the 1990s which aimed to formalise learning via a greater emphasis on certified learning were therefore highly controversial.

Formalising learning in the learning society

In Europe, policies of the 1990s placed a new emphasis on formal qualifications which included the expansion of tertiary education[7] and attempts to improve access to these qualifications. These policies were characterised by a sense of urgency, which stressed the need to raise the educational attainment of (mainly young) adults in order to ensure national competitiveness. Many institutions reorganised provision in order to meet the challenges. These organisational changes included the fostering of inter-institutional competition and the rapid expansion and greater diversity of the student population. These new imperatives were characterised by a concentration on learner or customer needs, flexibility in provision and learning processes and institutional accountability. The need to find new pathways into learning generated a renewed interest in informal or experiential learning and the ways in which this might be accredited by institutions.[8] The accreditation of prior experience or prior formal learning was to be used either as an entry qualification or as a means by which individuals could avoid having to repeat learning already undertaken informally (mostly learning in the workplace). Thus informal or experiential learning was being used either as a means of making formal learning more accessible, or as a means of accelerating routes to formal qualifications. These changes were ostensibly aimed at previously excluded groups, although it has in fact been used extensively by professional groups gaining new qualifications. In addition, aspects of the curriculum which had previously been part of 'informal' learning, such as career planning and personal development, were accredited with increasing frequency. This has potentially empowering effects for students who had traditionally been excluded in the past, to the extent that it values the experience of individual students and makes certification more accessible.

By the mid-1990s, a process of restructuring funding arrangements in the UK began with the withdrawal of funding from courses of learning that did not include formal certification as an outcome, making it difficult for institutions and local authorities to continue to offer some forms of informal learning. In adult education practice, particularly in university continuing education departments, these changes were unwelcome. Practitioners argued that students would be discouraged by the prospect of assessment and that the egalitarian relations fostered between students and tutors would be undermined by the introduction of assessment. Tutors feared that the curriculum would be constrained by the need to fit it into formal frameworks demanded by the funding councils and were concerned that the proposed changes were symptomatic of individualistic theories of learning, which many opposed. Others saw the mainstreaming of continuing education provision, such as access courses for those who did not have formal university entry requirements, as long overdue, arguing that university continuing education provision had largely failed to reach the most excluded social groups (Osborne, 2003).[9] Adult education courses were adapted and although assessment was often voluntary, it was taken up by students who were, according to evidence from a research study of the Open College Network, in England, pleased to receive formal certification (Davies, 2000).

Nevertheless, for some, these changes represented a shift away from adult education and towards lifelong learning and therefore an unwelcome change in social and political purpose (Martin, 2003). However, the point to note here is the gradual change in the locus of control and a propensity to focus on outcomes defined outside of the immediate learning environment. Here the focus had moved towards an emphasis on certification, increasing participation and targeting of particular groups. As in the rest of the public sector at this time, there was a growing emphasis on transparency and accountability which was realised in the development of NQFs and the refinement of funding mechanisms. This manifested itself in tighter regulation of credit level and content, and a technical focus on learning processes such as pre-specification of learning outcomes and assessment practices, as well as greater inter-institutional competition. This sometimes created conflicting motivations for institutions, such as concerns with competition and survival as well as widening access for students. This, in turn, resulted in variations in institutional responses and elite universities were sometimes slower to reform their practices than were other universities (Morgan-Klein and Murphy, 2002). The extent of such changes has varied between sectors within the UK education system and between national education systems.[10] However, what is relevant here is not so much the issue of institutional change but rather the shift towards formalised learning in policy and practice as a result of policies designed to accelerate the journey towards the learning society.

For the purposes of this discussion, the principal aim of these policies was to tackle social exclusion by increasing and widening access to qualifications and, at the same time, to increase the efficiency and accountability of the education system. Institutions responded to these objectives in different ways, producing a kaleidoscope of change (Morgan-Klein and Murphy, 2002). The accreditation of some informal learning did not result in the overnight collapse of the continuing education traditions in the older universities, as predicted, but the changes have remained controversial. It has been argued that an overemphasis on formal qualifications undermined the value of informal learning particularly in communities where it could play an important role in tackling social exclusion. In addition, methods of accrediting informal learning and specifying and measuring learning were regarded by some as regressive and criticised for having shifted the locus of control away from the immediate learning environment and out of the hands of both learners and teachers. This state of affairs is very far from the notion of learner-centredness. Moreover, the emphasis on formal learning risked classifying all of those engaged 'only' in informal learning as 'non-learners' (Coffield, 2000). At the same time, policies to widen participation in formal learning were having limited success in recruiting people from previously excluded groups. In the UK this has led to a renewed interest in informal learning and specifically in learning beyond the institution in communities.

Learning in the community

The character of community learning is highly context-specific for a number of reasons. First, it has been partly shaped by state social policies and welfare interventions and these differ significantly between nation states. Second, it is rooted in cultural and political traditions that are extraordinarily diverse throughout geographical areas and social groups. It is therefore difficult to make generalisations about community learning which account for these variations. We discuss 'lifelong learning' interventions in 'learning regions' across Europe in Chapter 9, but this chapter focuses exclusively on elements of community learning or community education in the UK.

The concept of *community* itself is ambiguous and requires clarification. Writing about community education practice in Scotland, Tett (2002) distinguishes between three meanings of community as it is used in relation to community learning. These are *place, interest* and *function*. Place is the most obvious meaning, referring to a community based upon a geographical area. Interest refers to a community of people who share the same goals or interests. These interests could be political, as exemplified by a campaign for improved services, or based upon shared membership of an organisation such as a church. There is often overlap between communities of interest and place. An interest in community also implies an interest in networks. The recent interest in social capital has renewed interest in the nature and quality of networks within which people engage and the way that this may impact on participation in learning and learning outcomes. Also, in the UK, communities are relatively segregated by socio-economic status and for those in the most deprived communities; networks are more likely to be local, which provides further illustration of the strong connections between place and interest, which are clearly both important and interrelated dimensions of community learning. The final area of meaning identified by Tett is that of function. This refers to the practice of community education – the professional groups and community representatives involved in community learning. As services in the UK become ever more integrated as in, for example, community schools in Scotland (McGonigal *et al.*, 2007; Scottish Office, 1998) or Children's Trusts in England (DfES, 2005), a diverse range of professionals and 'service users' or 'partners' are drawn together. For example, in community schools parents and children become active participants as well as a range of professionals such as teachers, social workers, health workers and community education practitioners of various kinds.

Since community learning is embedded in local communities and shaped by social and educational policy imperatives and local politics, a wide range of practices have been identified as relevant. Smith (1996, 2004) identifies a number of key terms associated with community learning. For Smith, *Community development* refers to increasing the capacity of particular communities through targeted resources for particular areas. *Community action* is understood as those actions which are taken by communities to promote change (tenant's groups would be a typical example). *Community organisation* refers to the collaboration and perhaps integration of services. Finally, *service extension* describes the way in which public services extend into communities – local authority 'one-stop advice and service shops' or health promotion activities in community schools, for example. This diversity of practice and the focus on deprived communities raises a number of issues for discussion here. First, what is the nature of relationships between members of communities and community learning professionals? Second, how relevant are developments in social policies in defining community learning activities? Third, how significant are alternative or oppositional models of practice. Finally, what are the trends in contemporary practice?

Tett (2002) cites Martin's typology of approaches to community education which include universal, reformist and radical models of practice. This typology highlights the issue of purpose and potentially differing perspectives in community education practice. The *universal* model assumes a basic consensus across communities and between professionals and communities. Here, the community educator's role is to make available non-selective provision for all. In the *reformist* model by contrast it is recognised that not all groups are able to access resources effectively and educational interventions are made on the basis that disadvantaged groups need most help. Finally, in the *radical* model, the central concern is with structured inequalities which systematically discriminate against some groups. This means that the role of the community educator is one of developing political education and community action in order to challenge existing arrangements. What these contrasting models highlight is that the purpose of community learning is contested regardless of whether or not it contains an overtly political dimension. Also the model of practice which predominates is likely to change over time and place.

Changing practices

In the UK in the second half of the twentieth century a reformist model of practice was highly significant perhaps predominant and had a strong compensatory ethic and practice. Typically, community education resources were targeted on areas in 'need' of community development. In the 1970s and early 1980s large-scale projects on this model were funded by local and national government. These interventions were known variously as Educational Priority Areas, Community Development Projects (CDP, 1977), Neighbourhood Renewal projects or Areas for Priority Treatment (Strathclyde Regional Council, 1979) and had some similarities with contemporary Education Action Zones in England.[11] These interventions were really a mix of social and educational activities designed to build capacity for community action and/or mitigate the effects of poverty and deprivation. The focus was on tackling the effects of poverty or social exclusion as it is now most often referred to. This was criticised as operating with a 'deficit' model of communities while at the same time ignoring the real problem which was identified as poverty and inequality. It was argued that such interventions could not succeed, often by practitioners operating within such projects but with a 'radical' understanding of practice, since they were merely compensatory and did little more than 'gild the ghetto' (CDP, 1977). Moreover, fiscal pressures throughout the period made projects on short-term funding soft targets for cuts in expenditure, which meant that such interventions were often short-lived. The significance of these interventions was first that debates over their efficacy highlighted the problematic role of practitioners in community settings who felt caught between the reformist and radical models of practice. Second, these social and educational interventions were embedded in essentially *social* policies and they highlight the vulnerability of learning in informal settings to changes in direction in *social* policy as well as in education policy.

Martin (2003) has drawn attention to contemporary changes in the direction of social policy and he argues that current policies on lifelong learning are implicated in the reform of the welfare state in the UK. This is similar to Field's (2006) argument that lifelong learning policies are, at least in part, an expression of the changing role of the state and in particular the changing relationship between the state and the individual. Martin argues that British social policy has evolved from a *welfare state* paradigm where there is at least a rhetorical emphasis on equity, through the *neo-liberal* approach of the 1980s emphasising individual competition and the efficacy of markets in distributing resources optimally, to the *Third Way* politics of the late 1990s and adopted by the New Labour Government in 1997. Third Way social policies are characterised by an emphasis on individual responsibility to take advantage of opportunities and to respond to the challenges of competition or suffer negative consequences (for example reduced benefit payments). There is a move away from state provision of services to one of the state as co-ordinator of a mixed economy of services utilising the private and voluntary sectors. If Martin is right, then we can expect to see features of *Third Way* politics in contemporary formulations of community learning.

In the Scottish Executive's (2004) *New Framework for Community Learning and Development* which sets out ways of working with communities, we see an emphasis on 'partnership' between public, private and voluntary agencies. These activities are coordinated through Community Planning Partnerships in line with national policy priorities and learning outcomes are to be linked to the Scottish Credit and Qualification Framework (SCQF). Arguably, this reduces the scope for communities to determine their own learning needs and desires. However, there is also an emphasis on dialogue with communities and mention of the importance of social inclusion, empowerment and self-determination and the need to target disadvantaged neighbourhoods. Finally, there is a concern with improving performance and the need to audit outcomes to ensure that partnerships are delivering efficiently. Desirable outcomes are expressed as 'social capital outcomes' and include,

- *More organised and influential communities*
- *More skilled communities with better access to education*
- *Communities with better access to resources and more control over assets*
- *More inclusive communities with wider involvement*

(Scottish Executive, 2004, 31)

Similarly, the contemporary reorganisation of community services for young people in England includes a mixed economy of services coordinated in part by Children's Trusts with an emphasis on efficiency and, in particular, information sharing between services (DfES, 2005). When considered with the 2007 proposals to make some form of education or training compulsory for 16–18 -year-olds (see Chapter 5), these changes give the state considerably increased powers over this age group in the form of enhanced information and tracking and sanctions for non-attendance at education or training placements. For Crowther (2004), contemporary developments demonstrate a tendency for *community as policy* to supplant *community as politics*. Community as policy is characterised by a 'top-down' agenda where desirable aims and outcomes are determined outside of the communities themselves. Community as politics, on the other hand, is characterised by greater community autonomy and alternative ideas outside and potentially in opposition to state politics and policies. Crowther, therefore, argues for a curriculum for social change which gives greater opportunities for voice, dialogue and dissent.

In summary, these examples emphasise the way in which the renewed interest in informal learning, at least in practice, is implicated in contemporary social policies. These developments raise difficult issues such as the tension between governmental emphasis on particular outcomes and the community's 'self-determination'. 'Partnerships' may also involve the exclusion of some groups where there are differences of perspective. For example, Tett (2002) notes in one of her case studies that parents and teachers had very different perspectives on how the school might operate to enhance community learning. In these ways, the processes and outcomes of informal learning in the community may have a disciplinary rather than an emancipatory effect.

Learning and the family

As in the renewed interest in community learning, lifelong learning discourses are implicated in a renewed concern with the family's links to learning outcomes for both parents and children. This includes recognition of the potential role that families play in creating social and cultural capital and the positive implications that this has for children's educational attainment. Governmental literature on families is permeated with the concern that families might be 'failing' in some ways either as a result of the social exclusion of vulnerable families or as a result of changes in family formations. Brassett-Grundy (2004a) notes that women with the lowest educational qualifications marry early and are most likely to experience early motherhood, while women with the highest educational attainment are least likely to marry at all. The increasing rate of divorce and rise in single parenthood households means that families are rapidly changing. In the UK, popular concerns about family life and in particular the perceived poor quality of parenting and misbehaviour of young people are a perennial topic in the mass media. Against this background, changes in the family are sometimes discussed in a utilitarian way as a potential threat to children's educational attainment. Writing in the OECD's *Schooling for Tomorrow* series, Carnoy (2001) is concerned that these changes may undermine the family's reproductive and productive capacity.

> In its ideal form, we envisage the family as an 'investment-production partnership.' ... the quality of upbringing has increased implications for future productivity and employability of the labour force ... Since parents will spend much of their time working outside the home, the services available to them to invest in their children will be key to how well the family does in its childrearing role.
>
> (pp. 126–127)

Carnoy advocates increased state support for families an example of which is the Sure Start programme[12] in England which aims to support parental employment and education aspirations by a variety of means such as encouraging uptake of childcare, delivering integrated services in children's centres and supporting parents in their parental role via outreach work and the distribution of various types of information. It is notable that Carnoy appears to take a normative view of the family indicating that it has an 'ideal form' and while the emphasis on changing family forms may be a legitimate policy concern; it is not the only or even the most important link between the family and education.

As far as the educational attainment of children is concerned (and this is a key governmental concern), the socio-economic status of parents is still the most accurate predictor of educational success or failure. The OECD results from PISA[13] show that children from lower socio-economic backgrounds do not receive the same educational opportunities as children from middle- and upper-class families. In many OECD countries schools actually reinforce these inequalities (OECD, 2006). This persistent inequality has been explained in a variety of ways.[14] Very broadly, these explanations can be categorised into those that emphasise cultural or social deficits in families whose children do not do well and those which emphasise processes, policies and practices that exclude working-class children. For example, Ball (2003) has explored the ways in which middle-class parents adopt choice strategies that maximise their own children's educational success. The current focus on increasing choice of schools and curricula in English education policy is trumpeted as placing power in the hands of students and parents. However, there is evidence that increased diversity of school type and curricula exacerbate between-school differences in student attainment (OECD, 2006). Ball's analysis suggests that this will adversely affect working-class children. Both deficit and exclusion explanations of educational inequality are concerned (in different ways) with the resources that families are able to draw upon in enabling learning within and beyond the family.

Current concerns with the social benefits of learning have led to a renewed interest in the links between social capital and educational attainment. In relation to the family, Field (2005) notes that in Northern Ireland 'bonding social capital' (found in traditional and localised networks) is linked with high educational attainment of young people but not with increased participation in adult learning. In assessing the role of social capital in families' relationships to learning, the problem of what to measure and how is acute. Croll (2004) uses the British Household Panel Survey data. This includes information on parental involvement with homework and the wider involvement of parents in organisations outside of the family. He makes a clear distinction between familial and non-familial aspects of social capital. Positive 'within family' processes such as greater involvement in homework monitoring appeared to be linked to higher GCSE results. Higher parental involvement in external organisations was also related to higher levels of attainment but he found that membership of external organisations was only weakly related to within-family processes such as involvement with homework and talking to children about things that mattered to them. He concludes that such 'within family' processes are relatively self-contained and only partly determined by social and economic circumstances. By contrast, McGonigal *et al.* (2007) writing about community schools in Scotland emphasise the agency of children in the ways that they move between networks themselves noting that children are highly competent in moving between formal and informal networks. The challenge for community schools, therefore, is to ensure that children have the opportunities themselves to generate social capital within community schools. Unfortunately, neither of these studies tells us much about adult learning.

These examples of research designed to identify and map crucial social processes in and beyond families highlight their complexities but they also suggest possible fruitful lines of inquiry. In particular, the issue of children's agency has been neglected in work on social capital and Field's research reminds us that there are clear links to be made between families and adult learning. Brassett-Grundy (2004a, 2004b) notes from her research on families and adult learning that while families may act as obstacles to participation in adult learning many families are supportive. Familial 'barriers' to learning in Brasett-Grundy's study included caring responsibilities, being in the process of forming a family and unstable living arrangements of various kinds. Some of these constraints are likely to be gendered. There is an extensive literature on the constraints placed on women's participation in adult learning though the familial issues faced by men are less well researched.[15] This brief overview presents a complex picture of the roles that families play in supporting learning and attainment. Social class and the resources families are able to access, such as social capital, are all highlighted in research. Investigating the ways in which families access and use such resources present researchers with particular challenges. Governmental interest in this is largely concerned with achieving particular outcomes such as improved educational attainment of young people or improved health outcomes for particular groups. Interventions here are likely to reflect this focus on 'community as policy' and indeed the funding of future research in this area. It seems likely that, as the population ages, governmental interest in the social benefits of learning, such as improved health outcomes will increase.

Concluding remarks

While lifelong learning policies were initially criticised for focusing on formal learning at the expense of informal learning, there has been increasing attention in recent years on the relevance of informal contexts such as the family and the community. The way in which learning in communities and families impacts on participation in formal learning and potentially brings social benefits, such as improved health outcomes, has been of central governmental interest. Interventions in community and family learning are likely to reflect current social policy imperatives which emphasise individual responsibility, a mixed economy of provision, accountability and projects defined by pre-specified objectives and outcomes. Lifelong learning discourses lend themselves easily to such an approach and are a long way from the idea of 'community as politics'. Nevertheless, the move away from the initial narrow focus on formal learning in formal contexts in lifelong learning policies and practices presents the possibility of a broader debate and revaluation of informal learning.

Notes

1 In this chapter we use the concept of *informal learning*. We argue that most learning episodes contain both formal and informal elements. Since our discussion focuses mainly on the impact of lifelong learning policies, practices and discourses, we are not here concerned with distinguishing between different learning processes. However, we discuss the meaning of informal learning in the chapter. See also Colley, Hodkinson and Malcolm (2003) for a useful and detailed review of the literature on this.
2 We discuss this further in Chapter 3.
3 Here non-formal learning is structured (perhaps through learning support) but normally takes place outside of institutions. Learners participate intentionally. Informal learning may be intentional but could also be accidental and arises out of everyday practices typically taking place in families or communities European Commission (2001) *Communication: Making a European area of Lifelong Learning a Reality*, cited in Colley, Hodkinson and Malcolm (2003).
4 We discuss the differences between individual and social theories of learning in Chapter 2.
5 See Crowther, Martin and Shaw (1999), Johnson (1979), Lovett (1988) and Fieldhouse (1996) on this. See Kane (2007) on popular education in Latin America. We discuss these issues further in Chapter 3.
6 We discuss social capital in more detail in Chapters 3 and 9.
7 We discuss this further in Chapter 6.
8 This is referred to as R/AP(E)L – recognition/accreditation of prior (experiential) learning. We discuss these trends in more detail in Chapter 7.
9 Simultaneous reform of local government in parts of the UK resulted in new efficiency imperatives which meant that funding which local authorities had previously made available for University Continuing Education courses was in many instances withdrawn.
10 See Young (2003) on the global growth of NQFs and Scott (1995) on audit mechanisms in higher education.
11 Education Action Zones are more narrowly focused on raising educational attainment in schools in designated zones. Office for Standards in Education (Ofsted) (2003) has published an evaluation of these.
12 See http://www.surestart.gov.uk on Surestart.
13 PISA is the Programme for International Student Assessment jointly developed by OECD countries and administered to samples of 15-year-olds in schools. This is discussed further in Chapter 5. See also http://www.oecd.org web pages.
14 See Reay (2006) and Cole (2006) for overviews
15 The relevance of caring relations is discussed in Chapter 3.

References

Ball, S. (2003) *Class Strategies and the Education Market: The Middle Classes and Social Advantage*. London: Routledge.
Baron, S., Wilson, A. and Riddell, S. (2000) Implicit knowledge, Phenomenology and learning difficulties. In Coffield, F. (ed.) *The Necessity of Informal Learning*. Bristol: Policy Press.

Davies, P. Formalising learning: The impact of accreditation. In Coffield, F. (ed.) *The Necessity of Informal Learning*. Bristol: Policy Press.

Brassett-Grundy, A. (2004a) Family life and learning: Emergent themes. In Schuller *et al.* (eds) *The Benefits of Learning, The Impact of Education on Health, Family Life and Social Capital*. London: Routledge.

Brassett-Grundy, A. (2004b) Family life illustrated: Transitions, responsibilities and attitudes. In Schuller *et al.* (eds) *The Benefits of Learning, The impact of Education on Health, Family Life and Social Capital*. London: Routledge.

Carnoy, M. (2001) Work, society, family and learning for the Future. *What Schools for the Future? Schooling for Tomorrow*. Paris: OECD.

Coffield, F. (2000) The Structure below the surface: Reassessing the significance of informal learning. In Coffield, F. (ed.) *The Necessity of Informal Learning*. Bristol: Policy Press.

Cole, M. (ed.) (2006) *Education Equality and Human Rights: Issues of Gender, 'Race', Sexuality, Disability and Social Class*, 2nd Edition. London: New York.

Colley, H., Hodkinson, P. and Malcolm, J. (2003) *Informality and Formality in Learning: A report for the Learning and Skills Research Centre*. London: Learning and Skills Research Centre.

Community Development Projects (1977) *Gilding the Ghetto: The State and the Poverty Experiments*. London: Community Development Projects.

Croll, P. (2004) Families, social capital and educational outcomes. *British Journal of Educational Studies*. 52(4): 390–416.

Crowther, J. (2004) 'In and Against' lifelong learning: Flexibility and the corrosion of character. *International Journal of Lifelong Education*. 23(2): 25–136.

Crowther, J., Martin, I. and Shaw, M. (eds) (1999) *Popular Education and Social Movements in Scotland Today*. Leicester: NIACE.

Davies, P. (2000) Formalising learning: The impact of accreditation. In Coffield, F. (ed.) *The Necessity of Informal Learning*. Bristol: Policy Press.

Department for Education and Skills (DfES) (2005) *Children's Trusts: Developing Integrated Services for Children in England National Evaluation of Children's Trusts*, Phase 1. Interim Report University of East Anglia in Association with the National Children's Bureau, Research Report RR617. London: HMSO

Fevre, R., Gorard, S. and Rees, G. (2000) Necessary and unnecessary learning: The acquisition of knowledge and 'skills' in and outside employment in South Wales in the twentieth century. In Coffield, F. (ed.) *The Necessity of Informal Learning*. Bristol: Policy Press.

Field, J. (2005) *Social Capital and Lifelong Learning*. Bristol: Policy Press.

Field, J. (2006) *Lifelong Learning and the New Educational Order*. Stoke on Trent: Trentham Books.

Field, J. and Spence, L. (2000) Informal learning and social capital. In Coffield, F. (ed.) *The Necessity of Informal Learning*. Bristol: Policy Press.

Fieldhouse, R. (ed.) (1996) *A History of Modern British Adult Education*. Leicester: NIACE.

Gorard, S., Fevre, R. and Rees, G. (1999) The apparent decline of informal learning. *Oxford Review of Education* 25(4): 437–454.

Johnson, R. (1979) 'Really useful knowledge': A radical education and working class culture, 1790–1848. In Clarke, J., Critcher, C. and Johnson, R. (eds) *Working Class Culture: Studies in History and Theory*. London: Hutchinson.

Kane, L. (2007) Conflict and co-operation between 'popular' and 'state' education in Latin America. *Journal of Adult and Continuing Education* 13(1): 53–67.

Lovett, T. (ed.) (1988) *Radical Approaches to Adult Education*. London: Routledge.

Martin, I. (2003) Adult education, lifelong learning and citizenship: Some ifs and buts. *International Journal of Lifelong Education* 12(6): 566–579.

McGonigal, J., Doherty, R., Allan, J., Mills, S., Catts, R., Redford, M., McDonald, A., Mott, J. and Buckley, C. (2007) Social capital, social inclusion and changing school contexts: A Scottish perspective. *British Journal of Educational Studies* 55(1): 77–94.

Morgan-Klein, B. and Murphy, M. (2002) Access and recruitment: Institutional policy in widening participation. In Trowler, P. (ed.) *Higher Education Policy and Institutional Change*. Buckingham: The Society for Research into Higher Education and Open University Press.

Office for Standards in Education (Ofsted) (2003) *Excellence in Cities and Education Action Zones: Management and Impact*. Manchester: Ofsted.

Organisation for Economic Co-operation and Development (OECD) (2006) *Education at a Glance 2006*. Paris: OECD.

Osborne, M. (2003) University continuing education in the United Kingdom. In Osborne, M. and Thomas, E. (eds) *Lifelong Learning in a Changing Continent*. Leicester: NIACE.

Reay, D. (2006) The zombie stalking English schools: Social class and educational inequality. *British Journal of Educational Studies* 54(3): 288–307.

Scott, P. (1995) *The Meanings of Mass Higher Education*. Buckingham: SRHE/OU.

Scottish Executive (2004) *Working and Learning Together to Build Stronger Communities: Scottish Executive Guidance for Community Learning and Development*. Edinburgh: HMSO.

Scottish Office (1998) *New Community Schools Prospectus*. Edinburgh: The Scottish Office, at http://www.scotland.gov.uk/library/documents-w3/ncsp-00.htm (accessed March 2007).

Smith, M/K. (1996, 2004) Community development. *The Encyclopaedia of Informal Education*, at http://www.infed.org/community/b- (accessed April 2007).

Strathclyde Regional Council (1979) *Room to Grow*. Glasgow: Strathclyde Regional Council.

Tett, L. (2002) *Community Education: Lifelong Learning and Social Inclusion*. Edinburgh: Dunedin Academic Press.

Young, Michael F. D. (2003) National qualifications frameworks as a global phenomenon: A comparative perspective. *Journal of Education and Work* 16(30): 223–237.

Chapter 9

Learning in the region

An initial response from many observers to the terms 'learning community', 'learning city' and 'learning region' or the plethora of other epithets that attribute agency to a geographically defined space is that it is people and not places that learn. This response, however, fails to recognise the fundamentally social nature of much learning and that learning occurs in a range of everyday settings in all sorts of places.

The learning city

It is certainly the case that an increasing number of initiatives around the world attribute to themselves the 'learning' or 'lifelong learning' prefix and do so from a range of perspectives. For example, in Germany, there are 71 learning networks that have been supported in a Federal learning region initiative and within these a huge variety of activities can be observed that cover the full range of provision that would be considered as lifelong learning (Federal Ministry of Education, 2004). Here the concept of a learning region appears to be broad-ranging and includes almost all activities that facilitate participation in the post-school period. All around the world there are municipalities that describe themselves as 'learning cities', 'learning towns' or 'learning villages'. Examples include Espoo in Finland, Victoria in British Columbia and Albury-Wodonga in New South Wales, and in many countries and provinces around the world the development is extensive and co-ordinated. For example, from 2001 in South Korea, 33 areas were designated as lifelong learning cities, including Chilton-gun, Kwanak-gu, Seongbuk-gu, Yangcheon-gu in Seoul, Kwangmyeong-si and Suncheong-si[1] and in the State of Victoria in Australia, the government has funded the development of 10 learning towns.[2] In the city of Hume, just outside Melbourne exists the Hume Global Learning Village linking a broad range of learning providers,[3] and we see the 'learning village' concept emerging in areas as diverse as Sweden (see Wallin, 2007), parts of Africa in the context of widening access to informal learning (see Boshier, 2006) and China (see Boshier and Huang, 2007).

Furthermore in many cases measures have been created of the extent to which geographical entities have achieved their 'learning' status. In Canada, for example, using the four pillars of UNESCO Commission on Education (1996) as the basis for measurement, the Composite Learning Index provides a comparative score for each city and region.

> Large cities across Canada are generally above the national average in all areas of learning, but particularly in the *Learning to Know* and *Learning to Do* pillars' . . . 'However, rural areas are stronger in their pillar scores for *Learning to Be* and *Learning to Live Together.*
>
> (Canadian Council on Learning, 2007)

Longworth (2006a) has usefully summarised the development of the learning city concept from its origins in the Organisation for Economic Co-operation and Development (OECD) (1973) initiative to establish the 'Educating City'. At that time, seven cities, Adelaide, Edmonton, Edinburgh, Gothenburg, Kakegawa, Pittsburgh and Vienna were invited by the OECD to become pilots in this programme with the objective of prioritising education within their strategic developments. As one of us has reported elsewhere (Sankey and Osborne, 2006), the term *Learning City* became the more common usage from the 1980s onwards. This subtle change from 'educating' to 'learning' emphasises the agency of the economic and social actors that make-up cities, and a more general tendency within the field of education in recent decades to acknowledge that individuals and organisations are not simply the objects of institutions, but shape their own learning paths. Useful parallels here may be drawn to ideas of self-directed learning, learning careers and learning trajectories that we introduced in Chapter 2. Each of these concepts signals the possibility for either individuals or organisations to assume agency in learning, although there is a conflicting picture of the extent to which self-determination of learning paths can or does exist. Learning Cities have themselves networked with each other. For example, the UK's Learning City Network includes over 80 members and itself provides one definition of what the concept means:

> Using lifelong learning as an organising principle and social goal, Learning Cities promote collaboration of the civic, private, voluntary and education sectors in the process of achieving agreed upon objectives related to the twin goals sustainable economic development and social inclusiveness.
>
> (DfEE, 1998)

Furthermore, at a global level we can also observe attempts to link cities and their stakeholders in networks (Longworth, 2006b).

The DfEE definition in itself contains some of the key notions that are integral to the Learning City concept: the responsibilities of a range of actors in facilitating learning; the creation of explicit and co-operative links between these actors; the goal of including all individuals irrespective of social and economic background, and especially those from groups historically excluded from access to learning opportunity; and a parallel commitment to economic development. The concept recognises that every sector contains learning resources.

It is important to note the twin concerns with both social and economic development, which have become commonplace in the rhetoric of lifelong learning and in its practice. As we emphasised in Chapter 4, often the two concerns of the social and the economic are falsely dichotomised and seen as conflicting objectives. However, for governments throughout the world social inclusion is a policy imperative alongside competitive economic development, and in the context of benefit to individuals of learning the link is clear. Creating the conditions for inclusion often relies on those economic developments that allow renewal of physical infrastructure, such as hospitals, colleges and schools. Partnerships at a local and regional level have been an important mechanism for these interventions, involving various mixes of public sector, private/commercial interests and community-based, non-profit organisations. The emphasis on partnership and mixed economies of services and resources reflects new approaches in *social* as well as in education policy, as we discuss in Chapter 8. Since most studies of participation in learning beyond school demonstrate that getting a job or promotion are key motivating factors, the close connection between the social and economic at the individual level becomes clear.

The European Union in its *Memorandum on Lifelong Learning* talks of transforming the concept of lifelong learning into 'concrete reality' and a little later within a set of projects that it funded under a programme entitled Regions of Lifelong Learning (R3L). It called for the

> mobilisation of all 'players' involved in ascertaining learning needs, opening up learning opportunities for people of all ages, ensuring the quality of education and training provision, and making sure that people are given credit for their knowledge, skills and competences, wherever and however these may have been acquired.
>
> (EC, 2002)

Once again there is an explicit emphasis on finding ways of engaging a range of agencies and decision-makers in creating learning opportunities. Co-operation and partnership between decision-makers, a variety of providers in the formal and non-formal sectors, social partners and citizens are emphasised in achieving this objective. It is also of interest in this quote that flexible opportunities for achieving credit is given some prominence. Here we see a link between community and individual agendas, and potentially conflicting emphases. The city and its agencies if working together in co-operative ways may create and maximise learning opportunities, but at an individual level, in order for a person to capitalise on their learning in the workplace, it is to be translated to a currency accepted by formal institutions and employers. This of course links to two features of modern systems of post-compulsory education: recognition and accreditation of prior learning (RAPL) and credit accumulation and transfer systems (CATS), which we explore elsewhere in Chapter 7.

Combining the economic and the social

A quote from the OECD illustrates the potential role of cities from a more strongly economic perspective:

> The city is dead. Long live the city! Those who have rushed to pronounce the city's demise in today's globalized communications world may have to eat their words. For cities (and their regions) can offer just the right mix of resources, institutional structures, modern technology and cosmopolitan values that allow them to serve as incubators and drivers for the knowledge-based societies of the 21st century.
>
> (Larsen, 1999)

Larsen argues that the Learning City concept is associated with theories about innovation and systems that promote innovation. In this model, a learning city or region puts innovation at the core of its development. The capacity to innovate, through adopting new approaches to problems and taking risks, is linked to the existence of infrastructures that allow for the collection, storage and transmission of knowledge and ideas, and the conditions that facilitate connections between key players engaged in economic development (see Florida, 1995). These connections, or forms of *social capital*, are intrinsic to *knowledge transfer* and economic performance.

Social capital has been explored already in Chapter 3. Briefly, it is about connections and ties between people. It is argued by many economists that highly dynamic regional economies capitalise upon their local assets at the regional level and in so doing, create competitive advantage (Cooke, 1997). Increasingly in modern economies that asset is knowledge and it is capitalised upon within social, cultural and institutional networks based upon mutuality and trust that thrive within regional settings where individuals and organisations are in close and frequent contact (Storper, 1997). Economic growth is increasing seen as being dependent on the quality of knowledge and diffusion of technology at a regional level. Regions become important since they are the spatial locus for interdependent clusters of researchers and innovators. Through the range of interactions that occur between the members of clusters (industry, government, NGOs, universities and their spin-offs companies, research institutes, Vocational Education and Training (VET) colleges and a range of other forms of organisations), there is a 'knowledge spill-over' that sustains the cluster. It is the network ties that squeezes knowledge out of the overall system and spreads it to places where it didn't trickle before. The implication for Cooke in the context of short cycle HE (quoted by Rosenfeld, 2000) is that this may 'necessitate a different form of community college, one that focuses on capabilities, encourages and rewards collaborative learning and the sharing of accumulated experience and knowledge – and perhaps even creates social settings and brokers relationships in which firms and other organizations also can learn from one another'.

It has been argued by Yli-Renko (1999) that social capital in inter-firm relationships improves access to external sources of learning, increases the willingness of firms to engage in dialogical interaction and improves the efficiency of the transfer and interpretation of knowledge.[4] Similarly it may also be the case in relation to connections between companies, where it is the existence of networks with both weak and strong ties that may be responsible for informal learning. Of course having access to learning based on that knowledge is not automatic, and at this point, it is important to note however that the connection between social capital and learning is complex. As Field (2005 a,b) points out, there is a positive association between social capital and educational attainment especially amongst the young, but the link between social capital and adult learning is weaker. Moreover, social capital is a distributed resource and some groups have stronger social capital than others.

The learning region

Larsen in his quote links the city and its region, and nowadays the terms *learning city* and the *learning region* are barely distinguishable in usage, and it is the concept of the *city-region* (cities with a surrounding hinterland) that is in common parlance (Charles, 2005). Region, like many terms is subject to a number of meanings. It may, for example, be a geographic area that encompasses a number of national political boundaries (e.g. the Middle East), one that crosses a number of regional political boundaries (the *Thames Gateway* in the South East of England), a particular unit of governance (e.g. Cape Province in South Africa – the *Learning Cape* (Walters and Etkind, 2004) or an area that is defined as a sphere of influence for its services by another agency. In the latter case, as Goddard *et al.* (1994) point out, in the context of the university, there are a range of geographic scales over which different types of services are provided. The local community or region differs according to whether the service is teaching, research or aspects of the third mission such as widening participation.

In essence, however, the idea of a *learning region* arguably simply extends the learning city in scale and scope and as in the R3L initiative refers to a region, city, urban or rural area, regardless of whether its identity is defined in administrative, cultural, geographical, physical or political terms. The further development of the lifelong learning regions as in the R3L initiative puts greater weight to the concept being inclusive of all within communities. The learning region also enables the recognition of the interaction and interdependence of the urban and rural, and presents the challenge of connecting the silos of urban policy and rural policy.

The emphasis on smaller geographical entities within which learning is situated links to broader issues of governance. Throughout the world we see a greater emphasis on regional and local levels of governance and the provision of services, including those of education and training 'close to the ground' (EC, 2000). According to Belanger (2006), it is at the level of urban communities and economic regions that individuals tend more to establish a local identity and rootedness. As a consequence, he argues that the 'growing sense of identity with the city creates a social demand for responsive regional or municipal government'.

We begin to see a number of facets and indeed interpretations of the learning region. These reflect differing emphases upon economic and social perspectives that have been taken by a number of authors. There is clearly no one definition of what constitutes a learning region, though Wolfe's (2002) contention, that the learning region provides the right institutional environment to promote private and social learning at four levels (individual; company; groups of companies; government) is a useful catch-all.

We might also ask how learning towns, cities and regions are distinguished from other forms of learning community. A recent report by Faris (2006) (see also Faris and Wheeler, 2006) in support of the Vancouver Learning City Initiative provides a helpful context. He argues that the term *learning community* can be utilised in a number of different ways and that it can refer to 'a community within a classroom or educational institution, a virtual global learning community, communities of practice, or those of place', and suggests that what we have been describing as learning cities and regions are part of a Russian doll of nested social learning environments of ever-increasing scale. As shown in Figure 1 below, each can be manifested in virtual form using information and communications technologies (ICTs) and each involves some form of two-way or multiple social interactivity between individuals. Learning neighbourhoods, villages, towns, cities and regions are what Faris describes as the *Learning Communities of Place*. He then argues that each type of community shares certain unique features as shown in Figure 9.1 and Table 9.1.

Elsewhere in this book, we consider communities of practice, many academic forms of learning community including schools, colleges and universities, learning organisational models and the role of ICT on a variety of levels within global contexts. The smallest unit, learning circles, described by Faris above refers to groups which self-manage their own learning. They are typified by a number of Nordic models as reported by Bjerkaker and Summers (2006) who distinguish these by their embodiment of democratic practice and their use of methods that allow citizens to better control their own destinies.

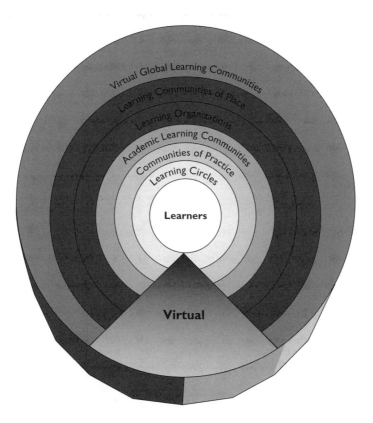

Figure 9.1 Learning communities: A nested concept of expanding scale and cascade of social learning environments (Faris 2006).

At this point we look at learning communities of place in practice. A number of authors provide examples including, most recently, Faris (2006), Longworth (2006a) and Duke, Doyle and Wilson (2006). It is possible from the work of these authors and from a multitude of other models of learning places around the world to suggest how principles underlying the concepts, we have previously described, are manifested in strategies, missions and actions.

We previously introduced some key features of the learning city, which we will now explore in more detail through investigating some concrete examples. These features are

- the responsibilities of a range of actors in facilitating learning
- the creation of explicit and co-operative partnership links between these actors
- social inclusion
- economic development.

Table 9.1 Learning communities: A nested concept of expanding scale and cascade of social learning environments.

Type	Scale (smallest to largest)	Example(s)	Unique Features or Characteristics
Virtual Global Learning Communities	**Largest**: World Wide Web networks of shared interest or purpose	*CISCO Academy of Learning *Commonwealth of Learning	Solely dependent upon Information and Communications Technologies (ICTs) e.g. Electronic Learning Communities
Learning Communities of Place	↑ **Civic Entities**: neighbourhoods, villages, towns, cities or regions	*Kent Learning Region *Victoria Learning City *Finnish Learning Villages	Place-based settings *Places that explicitly use lifelong learning as an organising principle and social/cultural goal *Political jurisdictions *Residents define operational boundaries *ICT used to network within and among learning communities of place
Learning Organizations	↑ Corporations/ Bureaucracies through to Small and Medium-sized Enterprises	*IKEA Natural Step Eco-Economic Model *UK Investors in People Scheme	Private, social or public enterprises that foster learning as a strategic objective *Shared Vision *Systems Thinking *Mental Models *Personal Mastery *Team Learning (Peter Senge, chief exponent)
Academic Learning Communities	↑ **Educational Institutions**: Colleges/ Classrooms	*Evergreen College *Community Schools	Formal education settings *Team Teaching *Interdisciplinary Approaches *Co-operative Learning (Meiklejohn, A., chief exponent)
Communities of Practice	↑ **Communities of Interest**: Professions, Trades, Avocations, etc.	*Artists' Workshop *Legal Assistants' Network	Initially solely face-to-face *Often Theme-based *Members are Practitioners *Members Learn from One Another (Etienne Wenger, chief exponent)
Learning Circles	↑ **Smallest**: Small groups engaged in learning activities of mutual interest	*Swedish Study Circle Movement *Small Group Discussions	Initially solely face-to-face *Small Group Dynamics *Optimum Size: 8–12 Persons (Kurt Lewin and Myles Horton, chief exponents)

Source: Faris (2006).

The range of actors

UNESCO has recognised for many decades that contributions to learning may be made by each of the five sectors that make-up our communities; civic, economic, education, public and voluntary. Table 9.2 shows examples of the contributions that each of these sectors might make to the learning city and the model presents learning within a *lifewide* as well as *lifelong* context. In short, learning is not something that simply occurs in formal or even non-formal settings: it is something that infuses all aspects of our lives. It is about our contribution to civil society, health and well-being, economic development, the environment and sustainability, rural and urban development and social/cultural development, and a number of agencies play a role.

There are clearly potential interconnections in practice between the sectors and purposes set out in Table 9.2, but how in practice are these actualised?

The creation of explicit and co-operative partnership links between these actors

The identification of a range of actors and their potentially linked contribution to the development of learning opportunity is one matter, but it is another matter to create meaningful and productive partnership. The development of effective partnerships is a key driver for encouraging and structuring community engagement at a variety of levels. It emerges as a key element in many successful initiatives around the world, and it is possible to identify facets of those partnerships that successfully mediate community engagement through a few illustrations.

In some societies, the approach to partnership includes at least an element of centralisation and even government legislation. In Scotland, for example, as a result of the Local Government in Scotland Act (HMSO, 2003), there is a statutory obligation on all local authorities to engage in 'Community Planning'. This very specifically requires the creation of structures that facilitate the engagement with communities in decision-making that affect the delivery of public services. In the regions of Scotland this has resulted in the setting up of Community Planning Partnerships (CPP) to address a range of linked issues, including Economic Development and Community Safety, Health and Wellbeing, and Lifelong Learning. In this model, local authorities are required to engage key players including Health Boards, Enterprise Networks, Colleges, Police, Fire Services and Transport Services in Community Planning at the regional level. It is not surprising that this and other similar attempts to bring together entities with common interests, but with separate organisation arrangements are described as being about *joined-up* service planning and delivery. At national level in Scotland, an agency of government, Communities Scotland, promotes community planning in the CPPs. This framework seeks, therefore, to balance high level oversight and integration of activity across sectors with mechanisms that allow for very local community participation. A concrete example of the combination

Table 9.2 A Learning city matrix: Examples of how a Community's sectors contribute to achieve shared objectives

Sectors	Purposes					
	Civic Learning	Health Promotion	Economic Development	Environmental Sustainability	Rural/Urban Development	Social/Cultural Development
Civic municipal government	* Citizen apprentices * Youth Advisory Council	* Community drug abuse strategy	* Farmers Market	* Green Belt initiative * Sustainable social housing projects * Local organic agricultural co-op	* Development of a Learning Quarter	* Tall Ships Festival * Learning Festival
Economic private to social enterprise	* Union shop steward training * Bd of Trade Election Forum	* Occupational health strategy * Migrant worker literacy	* Supply chain training strategy * Individual learning plans * Workplace literacy projects	* The Natural Step City strategy * Architects' Forum on sustainable design * Value-based Business Assn	* Vision 2020 initiative	* Artists' marketing co-op * Single Moms' catering company
Public libraries, museums, social/health agencies	* Library series on Rural-Urban Issues	* Community Early Learning Coalition * Seniors Centre health literacy	* Workplace health & safety program * Life Skills training	* Museum historical mapping project	* Library Learning Hub project	* Quality of life survey * Library Mother Goose program
Educational K to 12, post-secondary institutions	* College all-candidates meeting * School restorative justice program	* Student nurse community practicums	* Co-operative education projects	* Student river restoration project	* College urban planning seminar	* University International Students' Fair * Intergenerational service-learning
Voluntary Community civil society	* Community leadership training	* Night Youth basketball	* Disabled Assn food prep co-op	* Environmental movement lecture series * Community organic gardens	* Multi-faith social housing	* Multi-cultural festival * Family literacy * Faith Community kitchens

Source: Faris (2006).

of these approaches is provided by Parkin and Sankey (2005) in their description of the Community Futures programme in the Loch Lomond and Trossachs National Park. Here, they give an account of how community aspirations of local communities have been linked to the strategic planning for this area of natural heritage through creating the means for the views of communities to inform the development of policy and projects in the area. This work also demonstrates a link between lifelong learning and natural capital, our stock of environmentally provided resources and services (see Parkin, 2000). Conservation, sustainable use of resources, and sustainable economic and social development are a neglected part of lifelong learning actions, but clearly an understanding of the fragile condition of our ecosystem is viewed by many as *the* priority in education.

In Australia, in states such as New South Wales and Queensland, the attempt to secure collaboration amongst the many players involved in the provision of services at a neighbourhood, municipal or regional level tends to be referred to as place management. The objective in place management process is co-ordinated and integrated delivery of public services across all levels and sectors of government to specific geographic communities. Such models have been translated into Canada, for example in the establishment of Victoria, the capital of British Columbia, as a 'Global Learning City' in 2005.

Partnerships and collaborations need not be structured or initiated from above, and may develop spontaneously if conditions allow. Walters and Etkind (2004) describe the annual Learning Cape Festival in South Africa where within one month over 500 events are held, and it is because of the intense engagement of various actors that a range of networks and partnerships have been built. Irrespective of how partnerships in learning have come about, they do appear to have some common features. It would seem that a number of conditions are important not only in developing partnerships, but in sustaining them. These have been delineated by Wilson, Sankey and Osborne (2007) as clarity of outcomes, agreed and maintained governance arrangements, effective approaches to conflict resolution and clarity about the specific character of the contribution which particular partners are making.

Concluding remarks – Social inclusion and economic development once more!

We have already described initiatives in Chapter 6 that seek to include those, who for a variety of socio-economic reasons have been denied the opportunity to participate in learning, especially access to HE. The development of a regional approach has been the basis for a range of activity in this field since the late 1970s in the UK with most recently the creation of 'Aim Higher' and 'Lifelong Learning Networks' in England and 'Widening Access Fora' in Scotland.[5] Such arrangements tend to bring together educational providers (schools, vocational colleges and universities) and to a greater or lesser extent link with local or regional governments and non-formal providers in the planning of provision at a regional level. However, even if 'joined-upness' is achieved between separate sectors, simply offering access to educational provision will not combat inequity in itself since those who are excluded from education are also likely to experience multiple deprivation. In neighbourhoods with poor educational access and attainment, there will be higher unemployment, greater poverty and crime, and poorer housing, health and general quality of life. In England (in a similar way to the Scottish CPPs), this has been reflected in the creation of Local Strategic Partnerships (LSPs) in which statutory agencies and other actors on a voluntary basis work together in planning and in the delivery of services, and the Neighbourhood Renewal Grant (NRG) has been used to fund changes in service delivery in the most deprived areas. The logic is that the multiple forms of deprivation should be attacked in a cohesive way in order that neighbourhoods can be regenerated. Evidence of the success of such approaches is limited, but Shepherd (2006) reports that an investment to bring houses up to the 'Decent Homes Standard' in the South West of England is associated with a decrease in unemployment, improvement in education outcomes amongst the school-age population, improvement in health and reductions in crime.

Such developments are not without their critics. As we have pointed out in other chapters, the nature of partnerships formed is crucial if communities are to shape their own destinies as opposed to having these shaped for them. Moreover, the emphasis on social capital and social inclusion may sometimes be in tension with economic imperatives. Indeed, there is some cynicism about the current interest in social capital and it is argued that this is simply a case of economic interests wearing a community face (see Chapter 3). It is perhaps not surprising that the literature of learning regions is perhaps more influenced by economic rather than social considerations. As we have said earlier, it is argued that a particular set of conditions with a particular geography, especially the clustering of innovative companies are those that, from one perspective, create the foundations for a learning region. It is the development of their human capital (through amongst other things learning) and their connectivity (i.e. their social capital) that is the basis within this setting for the development of economic capital. We should at this point take care in relation to cause and effect. As Schuller (2000) points out, social capital is cited both as a *pre-condition* for social and economic progress and an *outcome* of it. In a flourishing community there may be many diverse networks in existence. Are they the cause of affluence or have they come about because of economic prosperity? There is perhaps less of a controversy in relation to human capital, and as we argue in Chapter 4 there is much evidence certainly at a personal level that investment in the development of skills and knowledge has a clear economic benefit (UUK, 2007).

In practice, where do we see the learning region delivering economic benefits? Nordic models are amongst the most persuasive in this regard. A combination of factors has ensured that the development of a knowledge-based economy is more reality than rhetoric. These include active central and regional government intervention. For example, in both Finland and Sweden the close links are mandated between the producers of knowledge (most particularly the universities) and its users, notably enterprises. In both countries the state requires universities to engage in 'third mission' activities, and they are funded to do so. At regional and city level in Finland, there has been a long-standing realisation of the need to build what Sotarauta (2005, 97) describes as the 'institutional foundation for future clusters and innovations'. He cites the example of Tampere, often referred to as the Manchester of Finland because of its industrial history (and its tall chimney stacks!), which through persuading two universities to move to the city in the 1960s created the knowledge base for the city to be part of the boom in ICT-related industries in the 1990s. His argument is that the ICT cluster of companies was complemented by universities that supplied knowledge and knowledge-workers.

We have noted the various ways in which there are new opportunities or new imperatives for formal learning organisations to work in partnership with other stakeholders – for example community schools and universities. In this way learning is increasingly less bounded. Nevertheless, there is still powerful stasis in the system. Sankey and Osborne (2006) have reported previously despite rejoiners to be part of a learning regions being found in many parts of the world, 'commitment to lifelong learning and/or their role at a regional level simply does not impinge on the consciousness of many organisations, especially schools and SMEs'. The Learning region as an overarching concept has considerable power to engage all potential stakeholders in collaborative activity based on partnership. However, there are also significant dangers for groups who have been excluded from decision-making in the past, since it is those with pre-existing network ties that are most likely to engage in new initiatives. The challenge here is considerable and the question of whether learning cities and regions can address both social and economic issues successfully is one that is as yet unanswered.

Notes

1 The Korean model is comprehensive and linked to the national *Comprehensive Life-long Learning Promotion Plan*, and Learning City status is achieved through a process of application. Of 57 cities that made applications in 2006, only 24 were selected. Different cities described as exhibiting 'best practice' focus on a varieties of issues including 'Social Integration', 'Traditional Culture Revitalization', 'Citizens' Community', 'Industry Innovation', 'Regional Innovation' and 'Learning Partnership' (See National Center for Lifelong Education, 2006).

2 These are Ballarat, Bendigo, Geelong, Horsham, Kyabram, Mt Evelyn, Wangaratta and Wodonga, and the Learning Towns within the Shires of Buloke and the Shires of Southern Gippsland (see http://www.acfe.vic.gov.au/comltown.htm)

3 See http://www.hume.vic.gov.au/Page/Page.asp?Page_Id=182&h=1

4 For a detailed overview of the relationship between SMEs, Social capital and learning, see Sorama, Katajamäki and Varamäki (2004).

5 For a full account of such arrangements, see Allen, Osborne and Storan (2006) and Osborne (2004).

References

Allen, L., Osborne, M. and Storan J. (2006) Literature review. Sub-theme 1: Local and regional partnerships to extend participation in higher education to socially disadvantaged groups. In Brennan, J., Little, B. and Locke, W. (eds) *Higher Education's Effects on Disadvantaged Groups and Communities* – A Report of an ESRC Network on Cross-regional Perspectives on the Transformative Impact of Higher Education on Disadvantaged Groups and Communities. London; CHERI, Open University.

Belanger, P. (2006) Concepts and realities of learning cities and regions. In Duke, C. Doyle, L. and Wilson, B. (eds), *Making Knowledge Work – Sustaining Learning Communities and Regions.* Leicester: NIACE.

Bjerkaker, S. and Summers, J. (2006) *Learning Democratically: Using Study Circles.* Leicester: NIACE.

Boshier, R. (2006) Widening access by bringing education home. In Oduaran, A. and Bhola, H.S. (eds) *Widening Access to Education as Social Justice: Essays in Honour of Michael Omolewa.* Amsterdam: Springer and UNESCO, pp. 23–43.

Boshier, R. and Huang, Y. (2007) Shuang Yu: Vertical and horizontal dimensions of China's extraordinary learning village. *Studies in Continuing Education* 29(1): 51–70.

Canadian Council on Learning (2007) *The Composite Learning Index – Helping Communities Improve their Quality of Life.* Ottawa: Canadian Council on Learning.

Charles, D.R. (2005) Universities and engagement with cities, regions and local communities. In Duke, C., Osborne, M. and Wilson, B. (eds) *Rebalancing the Social and Economic – Learning, Partnership and Place.* Leicester: NIACE.

Cooke, P. (1997) Regions in a global market: The Experiences of Wales and Baden-Württemberg. *Review of International Political Economy* 4(2): 349–381.

Department for Education and Employment (DfEE) (1998) *Learning Towns, Learning Cities – The Toolkit – Practice, Progess and Value.* Sudbury: DfEE, at http://www.lifelonglearning.co.uk/learningcities

Duke, C., Doyle, L. and Wilson, B. (eds) (2006), *Making Knowledge Work – Sustaining Learning Communities and Regions.* Leicester: NIACE.

European Commission (2000) *Memorandum on Lifelong Learning.* Commission Staff Working Paper, 30.10.2000. SEC(2000) 1832. Brussels: Commission of the European Communities.

European Commission (2002) *Call for Proposals (EAC/41/02) European Networks to Promote the Local and Regional Dimension of Lifelong Learning (The "R3L" Initiative).* Brussels: Commission of the European Communities.

Faris, R. (2006) *Learning Cities: Lessons Learning – A Background Paper Prepared for the Vancouver Learning City Initiative* (Unpublished). Vancouver, Canada at http://members.shaw.ca/rfaris/docs/VLC%20Lessons%20Learned.pdf

Faris, R. and Wheeler, L. (2006) Learning communities of place: Situating learning towns within a nested concept of social learning environments. Paper presented at Australian Learning Communities Network (ALCN) National Conference 2006 *Learning Communities,* 25–27 September, Brisbane, at http://members.shaw.ca/rfaris/docs/Learning%20Communities%20of%20Place.doc

Federal Ministry of Education (2004) *Learning Regions – Providing Support for Networks,* at http://www.bmbf.de/pub/learning_regions_providing_supports_for_networks.pdf

Field, J. (2005a) *Social Capital and Lifelong Learning.* Bristol: Policy Press.

Field, J. (2005b) Social networks, innovation and learning: Can policies for social capital promote both dynamism and justice? In Duke, C., Osborne, M. and Wilson, B. (eds) *Rebalancing the Social and Economic – Learning, Partnership and Place.* Leicester: NIACE.

Florida, R. (1995) Towards the learning region. *Futures,* 27(5): 527–536.

Goddard, J., Charles, D., Pike, A., Potts, G. and Bradley, D. (1994) *Universities and Communities.* London: CVCP.

Her Majesty's Stationery Office (HMSO) (2003) *Local Government in Scotland Act.* Edinburgh: HMSO.

Larsen, K. (1999) Learning cities: The new recipe in regional development. *OECD Observer,* August 1999, p. 73.

Longworth, N. (2006a) *Learning Cities, Learning Regions, Learning Communities: Lifelong learning and Local Government.* London: Routledge.

Longworth, N. (2006b) *City Rings – A Strategy for Enhancing Lifelong Learning in Cities and Regions through International Links between Stakeholders,* at http://www.obs-pascal.com/docs.php?doc=167.

National Center for Lifelong Education (2006) *Lifelong Learning City,* at http://www.lll.or.kr/eng/llc/llc_01.php.

Organisation for Economic Co-operation and Development (OECD) (1973) *Recurrent Education: A Strategy for Lifelong Learning.* Paris: OECD/CERI.

Organisation for Economic Co-operation and Development (OECD) (2001) *The Wellbeing of Nations: The Role of Human and Social Capital.* Paris: OECD.

Osborne, M. (2004) Adults in British higher education. In Mark, R., Pouget, M. and Thomas, E. (eds) *Adults in Higher Education: Learning from Experience in the New Europe.* Oxford: Peter Lang.

Parkin, S. (2000) Sustainable development: The concept and the practical challenge. *Civil Engineering,* 138: 3–8.

Parkin, S., and Sankey, K. (2005) Sustainable development. In Duke, C., Osborne, M. and Wilson, B. (eds) *Rebalancing the Social and Economic – Learning, Partnership and Place.* Leicester: NIACE.

Rosenfeld, Stuart A. (ed.) (2000) *Learning Now: Skills for an Information Economy.* Washington DC: American Association of Community Colleges, Community College Press, pp. 4–5.

Sankey, K. and Osborne, M. (2006) Lifelong learning reaching regions where other learning doesn't reach. In Edwards, R. *et al.* (eds) *Researching Learning Outside the Academy.* London: Routledge.

Schuller, T. (2000) Social and human capital: The search for appropriate technomethodology. *Policy Studies* 21(1): 25–35.

Shepherd, C. (2006) 'Regenerating communities – or "the poor are always with us": A UK experience'. In Duke, C., Doyle, L. and Wilson, B. (eds) *Making Knowledge Work – Sustaining Learning Communities and Regions.* Leicester: NIACE.

Sorama, K., Katajamäki, A. and Varamäki, E. (2004) *Co-operation between SMES: Social Capital and Learning Perspective.* 13th Nordic Conference on Small Business, at http://web.bi.no/forskning/ncsb2004.nsf/23e5e39594c064ee852564ae004fa010/a6cb7066ea59eda6c12567f30056ef4d/$FILE/Sorama&al.pdf

Sotarauta, M. (2005) Tales of resilience from two Finnish cities: Self-renewal capacity at the heart of strategic adaptation. In Duke, C., Osborne, M. and Wilson, B. (eds) *Rebalancing the Social and Economic – Learning, Partnership and Place.* Leicester: NIACE.

Storper, M. (1997). *The Regional World*. New York: The Guildford Press.

UNESCO Commission on Education (1996) *Learning The Treasure Within*. Report to UNESCO of the International Commission on Education for the Twenty-first Century. Paris: UNESCO.

Universities UK (2007) *Research Report: The Economic Benefits of a Degree*. London: UUK, at http://bookshop.universitiesuk.ac.uk/downloads/research-gradprem.pdf.

Wallin, E. (2007) Place centric and future oriented learning in the local village context. In Osborne, M., Sankey, K. and Wilson, B. (eds) *Social Capital, Lifelong Learning and the Management of Place: An International Perspective*. London: Routledge.

Walters, S. and Etkind, R. (2004) *Developing a Learning Region: What Can Learning Festivals Contribute?* Paper Presented at the AERC Conference, Victoria, Canada.

Wilson, B., Sankey, K. and Osborne, M. (2007) Conclusion. In Osborne, M., Sankey, K. and Wilson, B. (eds) *Social Capital, Lifelong Learning and the Management of Place: An International Perspective* London: Routledge.

Wolfe, D. (2002) Social capital and cluster development in learning regions. In Holbrook, J. A. and Wolfe, D. (eds) *Knowledge, Clusters and Regional Innovation: Economic Development in Canada*. Kingston: School of Policy Studies, Queens University, pp. 11–38.

Yli-Renko, H. (1999) Dependence, social capital, and learning in key customer relationships: Effects on the performance of technology-based new firms. *Acta Polytechnica Scandinavica*. Industrial Management and Business Administration, Series No. 5. Espoo: The Finnish Academy of Technology.

Chapter 10

Information and communication technology and lifelong learning

Introduction

A key element of lifelong learning as discourse is the notion of flexibility which we discuss in Chapter 1. Flexibility of provision includes, meeting students' needs at times and places, and at a pace of their own (or their employers') choosing. The availability of open and distance learning opportunities based on the use of information and communications technologies (ICTs) has been heralded as being especially important in achieving this flexibility. The growing use of ICT in teaching and learning means that long-sstanding assumptions about the relationship between time, place and learning are breaking down. ICT means that not only learners do not have to attend a particular place, they also do not have to learn at particular times or in particular ways. Courses can be taken in the home, in the workplace or at any location remote from a learning provider, who could be next door or in another continent (or both since increasingly different institutions are collaborating in providing courses collaboratively[1]). For the advocates of ICT, these approaches represent a movement in the locus of control from teacher and institution to the learner, who through the flexibility of new technology can make self-directed learning a reality. Futhermore, it has been argued that the connectivity that the Internet brings also increases individuals' stock of social capital, both of a bonding and a bridging form.[2] It brings individuals together with those they know, but creates bridges to others, and aids the development of socially sustainable communities (see Timms, 2007).

These developments are linked to other themes that we have already considered. Technological developments in ICT are integral to the development of the *Knowledge Society*, which is central to economic change. The resources of the World Wide Web (WWW) and the interactivity within it are an unprecedented reservoir of knowledge. The growth of ICT is also important in the *globalisation* of lifelong learning. Institutions across the globe are marketing their courses to individuals thousands of miles away and linking with institutions in other countries in order to provide courses to disparate groups and individuals.

Whilst much of this activity is provided by colleges and universities with long-standing traditions and some specialist providers of distance education, it is also the case that the increased use of ICT has been paralleled by the creation of new forms of providers. Several new institutions have emerged, most notably Pheonix University,[3] offering online programmes. What distinguishes these universities from traditional Open Univeristies such as the UK Open University is their rapid growth and range of offer, in particular their focus on short CPD programmes. The increasing commodification of education across the world has also led to private, multinational corporations becoming increasingly significant players in education in general and lifelong learning in particular. Even at the end of last decade, Moore (1999) was writing about more than 'a thousand other corporate universities, including the IBM Global Campus, Motorola University, Sun Microsystems University and the World Bank's Economic Development Institute', offering specialist provision both as CPD to their own staff and to external customers.

Furthermore, many corporations are now active in the education market offering electronic toys and games with an educational function. They are able to draw upon resources which the vast majority of universities, let alone smaller colleges, can only dream about. As a result, there is now a blurring between education and entertainment (*edutainment*) that parallels the convergence between Internet and broadcast technologies.

ICT has been viewed as an important feature within the two key strands within lifelong learning policy of social inclusion and economic competitiveness (Gallacher, Osborne and Cloonan, 1999). It has the potential to enhance social inclusion by making learning available to unprecedented numbers of people in all sorts of geographic locations at a time when many societies are moving towards the massification of post-compulsory education. It also provides opportunities for those excluded for reasons of mobility and a range of disabilities. Second (and sometimes concurrently), it can enhance competitiveness by using technology to reduce costs, and provide the means for those in work to access learning more readily. ICT also provides the means whereby individuals in the workplace can engage collaboratively with others within and outwith occupational, professional and organisational boundaries without the limits of time, place or pace. Furthermore, many advocates of ICT point to its potential advantages for teaching and learning with those from the *social contructivist* school of learning in particular arguing for its advantages (see Jonassen, 1998). Many in this school would argue that whilst learning is an individual act it is expressed in and through social processes, and that information and communications infrastructures provide rich possibilities for social interaction.

However, there are potential downsides. Cost is of course still a barrier, and whilst we envisage in OECD countries ever-expanding possibilities the reality despite advances in satellite technology in parts of the world is of an every increasing 'digital divide'. Ferlander and Timms (2001) have argued that whilst differences in access to information have always characterised human societies, what is distinctive about the early twenty-first century is the importance of information in participating in a rapidly changing society. These differences are not simply between the OECD countries and the rest, though clearly there are greater challenges for the poorer nations (see, for example, Ahmed and Nwagwu, 2006). Initiatives such as the UN's 2006 initiative, the Global Alliance for Information and Communication Technologies and Development (GAID) recognise the importance of ICT in relation to the achievement of its Millennium Development Goals (MDGs) (UN, 2000), and has been created to address key global issues related to ICT in development. Amongst these is broadband connectivity, particularly in Africa, where in many areas telephony service is not available (see GAID, 2007).

Even within the richer countries there have been fears that digital divides may develop between socio-economic groups. A clear concern has been that technologically deterministic approaches using ICT would be viewed as *the* solution to improving inequities in participation due to location or mobility (see Gorard and Selwyn, 1999). The European Commission's Memorandum on Lifelong Learning Key message 6: Bringing learning closer to home of the Memorandum on Lifelong Learning is typical of the hopes placed upon ICT: 'Developing innovative teaching and learning methods in which ICT-based technology is an integral part. . . . To provide lifelong learning opportunities as close to learners as possible, in their communities and supported through ICT-based facilities wherever appropriate' (EC, 2001).

By contrast to this optimism, concerns have been that an IT-literate would emerge, and that ICT would be the preserve of an elite. Rather than being part of the solution to concerns about inclusion, ICT would be part of the problem unless policy makers recognised that technological solutions would have to be accompanied by realistic opportunities to access learning that take into account the multitude of barriers to learning that many experience. Nonetheless, whilst it is undeniable that there are divisions in access to technology, perhaps these fears underestimated quite how prevalent new technologies would become, and how relatively low in cost (at least in some countries) both hardware and access would become.

Concerns have also been expressed at the capacity of ICT to engage learners in quite the way some optimists might have suggested. The Virtual Learning Communities (VLCs) of the Internet may display some of the features of more traditional Learning Communities, but the forms of interactivity which up until this point have been possible have meant that some of the features of face-to-face interaction have neither been replaced nor augmented by ICT. To take but one example, the use of videoconferencing (VC) has been rejected by many teachers on pedagogic grounds, but its failure has largely been due to technical inadequacies (see Pechey, 2006). Lack of reliability of connections, low bandwidth leading to poor audio and picture quality and lack of functionality of equipment and infrastructure have all led to frustration for teachers. Students, taking their norms from television, have additionally been frustrated by the presentational skills of teachers. As the technology improves, then the limitations of VC as a form of delivery for lectures, seminars and tutorials or for less structured learning episodes perhaps will be no greater than those of equivalent face-to-face situations. Other communications tools embedded in Virtual Learning Environment (VLEs) have also improved and offer multiple functionality through one platform readily accessed at a single website. It will be no longer possible to blame the tools as VLEs such as Blackboard™ become ever more easy to use. Furthermore, there is plenty of online advice on the use of technology that is readily accessible (see, for example, videoconferencing in Education).[4]

The generations of flexible learning

ICT and *e-learning* are used almost synonmously, but they refer to a range of technologies with various degrees of interactivity between teacher and learner, and between learners themselves. Taylor (1996) usefully summarised what he then described as the four generations of distance education and flexible delivery as shown in Table 10.1.

It is the fourth generation, much of which has developed as a viable pedagogical form in the last decade, that now dominates within flexible learning. Internet technologies provide unprecedented access to resources within the World Wide Web, and various communications platforms allow both synchronous and asynchronous communications via text, audio and video. Rapidly over this time, we have seen in many countries, costs of accessing these resources decline and the

Table 10.1 Flexible delivery technologies – a conceptual framework

Models of distance education and associated flexible delivery technologies	Characteristics of flexible delivery technologies				
	Flexibility			Highly Refined Materials	Advanced Interactive Delivery
	Time	*Place*	*Pace*		
First generation – The correspondence model					
Print	Yes	Yes	Yes	Yes	No
Second generation – The multimedia model					
Print	Yes	Yes	Yes	Yes	No
Audiotape	Yes	Yes	Yes	Yes	No
Videotape	Yes	Yes	Yes	Yes	No
Computer-based learning (e.g. CML/CAL)	Yes	Yes	Yes	Yes	Yes
Interactive video (disk and tape)	Yes	Yes	Yes	Yes	Yes
Third generation – The telelearning model					
Audioteleconferencing	No	No	No	No	Yes
Videoconferencing	No	No	No	No	Yes
Audiographic communication	No	No	No	Yes	Yes
Broadcast TV/radio and audioteleconferencing	No	No	No	Yes	Yes
Fourth generation – The flexible learning model					
Interactive multimedia (IMM)	Yes	Yes	Yes	Yes	Yes
Internet-based access to WWW resources	Yes	Yes	Yes	Yes	Yes
Computer mediated communication.	Yes	Yes	Yes	No	Yes

Source: Taylor (2006).

speed at which they are accessed increase. In the UK, for example, it is estimated that one in two households have broadband, allowing fast downloads of material to home computers and continous access to resources and other individuals for relatively low costs.

Virtual learning environments

VLEs are the ubiquitous form that the fourth generation takes and are the basis for the flexibility of a considerable proportion of lifelong learning offered through formal and non-formal education providers. A VLE such as WebCT is an online environment that integrates a range of information and communications tools in a single virtual location. With hardware of the appropriate quality, learners are able to receive learning materials via text, audio and video, and can interact via a range of forms of asynchronous and synchronous communications through email and real-time chats via text, audio and video with one or more others. These interactions can be made from any place where a connection to the Internet can be made; with the increasing prevalence of wireless broadband, those numbers of potential places is increasing. Where synchronicity isn't necessary for communication and interaction, time and pace of interaction is also stretched.

By 2001, Taylor was talking about *fifth generation* distance education with reduced and potentially no tutor input. Here, he was referring to prototype 'intelligent object databases' that would order the many valuable comments made in electronic discussion groups by teachers and students and then could be interrogated by students using key words. When the system receives an electronic query from a student, 'the search engine seeks an appropriate match with a previously asked question, which if successful, triggers a personalised response to the current question without concurrent human intervention' (Taylor, 2001, p. 7). However, despite the optimism that such models would also advance the scaling up of provision whilst maintaining interactivity, development appears to have stalled and whilst the technology has been useful for handling administrative queries but has not proved robust for teaching and learning.

Such has been the rapidity of advance in technology, we now have moved beyond e-learning to m-learning. It is now becoming commonplace for mobile handheld devices to handle not only telephone calls and text messaging, but also, using GPRS, email, synchronous audio and videoconferencing and the download of large documents. Providers of mobile technologies now routinely speak of the equivalent of whole encyclopaedias being available on handheld devices and in the future most of that which has been ever produced in print, audio or video form being accessible. It is predicated that digitally broadcast live TV will routinely be available on handhelds within a decade, and there will be increasing convergence of devices that offer one or more of the facilities of MP3 players, digital cameras and video-recorders, wireless Internet and *de facto* radio and TV (see Anderson, 2005).

Teaching and learning principles

There is much material available on the WWW, some very expensive to access and most free.[5] A simple trawl using a search engine and almost any set of key words will reveal multiple links to web pages. But how are we to distinguish in this treasure trove material that is of quality from the rest, and how are we to learn from these resources? One of the rhetorics of lifelong learning is the capacity to be a self-directed learner, one who, taking Candy's (1991) interpretations of this concept, has the capacity to be autonomous, self-managing and in control of their own personal learning path. Never before has there been such enormous potential for this to be realised. In principle, the Internet is a haven for the autodidact, but most of us need at least a little guidance in our learning. However, most resources have not been designed as learning vehicles, and many that have do not display many of the fundamental principles of good pedagogical design. Some materials of course are made available to aid learning, and have no pretensions to being part of a teaching programme. Print material in the form of books, journal articles, conference papers, transcripts of speeches and much more, as well as a raft of audio and video material can be sourced readily and often the originators of that material envisage a use in teaching and learning. It is quite a different matter, however, to embed such material within a structured programme.

One model of programme design appears to dominate in the pedagogy of e-learning, that based on principles of social constructivism, and this model has in particular application in the case of mature learners, already possessing some expertise relating to the content of the material under consideration. Hung and Chen (2001) have suggested four principles for the design of e-learning that serve as a useful starting point for considering what features such programmes developed from this perspective might include. We will consider the extent to which these principles accord with understandings of lifelong learning.

Hung and Chen's principles of design are *commonality, situatedness, interdependency* and *infrastructure* and are based on principles that emerge from situated cognition and the work of Vygotsky (1978) (Table 10.2). Commonality refers to the concept that learning occurs through participation in social communities, and in constructing and developing identity within these communities. It is associated with the membership of a *community of practice*,[6] a term made popular by Lave and Wenger (1991, p. 98) as '. . . an activity system about which participants share understandings concerning what they are doing and what that means in their lives and for their community'.

They further define a community of practice as one within which a set of individuals are united both in action and in the meaning that the action has, both for themselves and for the larger collective. It is this commonality that gives them a good and valid reason to work together. Communities of practice may be related to a specific occupational context and are widely linked to workplace

Table 10.2 Selected principles for e-learning

Principles of situated cognition and Vygotskian thought	Principles of online teaching and learning
Commonality Learning is a social act leading to identity formation and associated membership of a community of practice.	E-learning environments should capitalise on social and collaborative communication with others who have shared interests.
Situatedness Learning is reflective, metacognitive and embedded in rich socio-cultural contexts.	E-learning environments should enable students to work on activities and projects that demand reflection on authentic practice.
Interdependency Learning is socially mediated and facilitated through engagement in practice with others.	E-learning environments should generate interdependencies that benefit from the diverse expertise in the learning community.
Infrastructure Learning is facilitated by activity, accountability and associated support mechanisms.	E-learning environments should incorporate facilitating structures, accountability mechanisms, and associated rules of engagement.

Source: Taylor (2002), adapted from Hung and Chen (2001).

learning (see Allan and Lewis, 2006), but are also cited in connection with many and various others sites of formal and non-formal learning.

Postle *et al.* (2003, 108) describe how this commonality plays out in e-learning environments at the University of Southern Queensland in Australia

> For example, in some courses students create subgroups based on similar work contexts (schools, industry trainers, ESL teachers, vocational education teachers). In other courses, this was taken further when assessment schemes demanded project-based authentic assessment (in groups), peer review of one another's work and reflection on action.

Situatedness is defined by Hung and Chen (2001, 7) as 'when learning is embedded in rich situations and social constructive acts'. Thereby meaning can be made extracted 'in the contexts of application and use' with learners picking up 'both implicit and explicit knowledge'.

A valuable learning environment is thus one that situates learning within authentic practices and engagements with others within the community that engages in these practices. Learning *then* has a real context within which existing knowledge is tested and new knowledge emerges.

Interdependency refers to participants within a learning group taking advantage of the different strengths of individuals using diversity in a positive manner. The features of both situatedness and interdependency are well illustrated in a case study of an online programme described by Timms (2007, 71)

> Participants were required to work collaboratively in small groups in order to produce comparative 'portraits' of the communities in which they worked. Participants were expected to use their cultural and individual differences of perspective to sharpen each other's awareness of their community and to explore the positive as well as any negative features. The collaborative process was also expected to enhance the participants' awareness of their own, as well as each other's, perceptual frameworks and to encourage them to recognise the advantages of collaboration for extending ways of gathering and interpreting information, deepening understandings and developing ideas and innovations. Each participant was a looking glass for the others.

Infrastructure refers to 'rules and processes, accountability mechanisms and facilitating structures' (Hung and Chen 2001, 9). Rules and processes refer not only to the sorts of behaviours that are expected of students in an online environment ('netiquette'), but also the atmosphere that teachers seek to create. Potential desirable behaviours such being encouraging, supportive and reflective and working as part of a team can of course be modelled by the teacher, but a good deal of more explication will be necessary in an online environment than in face-to-face situations so that all members will have a clear idea of roles and expectations.

Hung and Chen's model and others who take similar perspectives, whilst dominant in the field of ICT, are not necessarily the only approaches to take. Nor do they necessarily accord with some ways in which we might interpret being a lifelong learner. This predominant approach stresses being part of a community, collaboration and interdependence. There can be no doubt that these features may be desirable, but they are not necessarily the preferred approach of all learners, and certainly would not figure as features of some models of the independent self-directed learner. The element of design that stresses interdependence is perhaps the most contentious since it depends on co-operation between individuals and the subjugation at least to a certain degree of individual need to the needs of others in the group.

Whilst the diversity that different individuals bring to a group may be enriching, behaviours in online learning environments would suggest that some individuals contribute more wholeheartedly than others. Our experience as teachers in online environments over some years suggests that like many of the aspects of interaction that have been promoted as the benefits of online learning, beliefs that learners will necessarily wish or are able to interact frequently tend to be idealist. Lack of interaction may be because of a preference for a particular *learning style* or teaching method or simply because circumstances dictate that interaction is not possible because of constraints of time, location or technology.

We have used the term *learning style*, but are well aware of the pitfalls that this concept carries, because the lack of validity of many of the instruments (usually questionnaires) that are used to determine preferences.[7] Some tools do stand up to scrutiny, but even then a range of questions emerge. A much-cited implication of having been able to establish a preferred learning style is that teachers should then adopt a particular teaching approach. This is replete with difficulties. As Tennant (1997) has pointed out, how could we ever design an approach that would meet the different preferences of a multitude of learners? And is it desirable to even do so? Exposing learners to approaches that they are uncomfortable with or even dislike might create greater dividends because of the cognitive dissonance that it engenders. Postle and Sturman (2003) have considered the sorts of behaviours that occur amongst online learners and speak about 'lurkers', who observe, but do not otherwise engage in online environments. What seems clear is that just like learners in any learning environment, those engaged through ICTs exhibit equivalent and varied behaviours. If our ethos is that lifelong learners are self-directed beings, then coercion to learn in a particular fashion would be anathema. With such thoughts in mind, prescribing *an* approach to learning would make no sense. Similarly, whilst there are may be benefits in learning from the commonality that a community of practice creates so are there from engagement with those with whom there are clearly conflicting perspectives. Furthermore, many arrangements that label themselves as communities are rather exclusive and are close to particular individuals, especially those based around the workplace. Rather than encouraging an expansive form of learning, they may seek conformity and consensus amongst members who are directed towards goals that are determined by corporate rather than individually determined need (see Hodgson and Reynolds, 2005). Lave and Wenger (1991) and those who firmly sit within the school of situated learning, stress how learning occurs through participation in communities of practice, and how new and authentic knowledge is created in practice. Others have emphasised the relevance of internal psychological processes as stressed in traditional cognitive (and indeed behaviourist) models of learning. Theoretical understandings of learning processes are highly contested. This is not just a matter of a focus either on the individual or the social aspects of learning. Tennant (2006, p. 113) in a recent overview of what he describes as two opposing traditions of cognitive psychology, cognitive structuralism and information processing, points to the theoretical tensions on

> the role of individual knowledge within a community of practice, the degree to which knowledge can said to be generic and context independent, the ways in which knowledge can be utilized in new situations, and the processes through which knowledge is incorporated or disbursed among individuals in a community.

There is a danger in accepting one theoretical position with regard to what is the best approach to learning as Illeris (2002) illustrates, again using the metaphor of tension, in his case between its cognitive, emotional and social aspects.

Concluding remarks

Rather than proposing 'one approach fits all in learning using ICT', it may in the end be more profitable to think simply about 'alignment' in teaching and learning frameworks in the sense of Biggs' (1999) model. His model (applied to teaching and learning generally) seeks simply to constructively align learning objectives, assessment tasks and teaching methods. It is clear that if designers take into consideration the objectives of programmes more clearly, then courses will assume greater fitness for purpose. In Mayes' categorisation of courseware in the context of ICT and lifelong learning, he speaks of three levels: primary, secondary and tertiary, each relating in general terms to content, activities and discussion, respectively.

> Primary Courseware is intended mainly to present subject matter. It would typically be authored by subject matter experts but is usually designed and programmed by courseware specialists. Increasingly, primary courseware will be web-based. Secondary Courseware describes the environment and set of tools by which the learner performs learning tasks, and the tasks (and task materials) themselves. Tertiary Courseware is material which has been produced by previous learners, in the course of discussing their learning tasks with peers or tutors. It may consist of outputs from assessment.
>
> (2002, p. 5)

Wellman (2001) describes behaviours within the Internet as *networked individualism*, with users of such technologies having few links to local groups, but being tied strongly to more geographically spread networks. ICT can also be viewed as providing an environment where for the first time lifelong learners have the opportunity not only to engage with material constructed by 'experts' (the primary level), communicate and interact with others (the secondary level), but also contribute their expertise and learn from the expertise of peers (the tertiary level). If we take ICT to be no more than 'shovelware' (placing huge amounts of text on the web) then one instructional model pertains. This may be appropriate in some cases and indeed is likely to be viable for a number of education and training purposes, and probably the most financially robust model. Furthermore, blended learning approaches that combine ICT and some face-to-face learning may be desirable development of this primary level. If, however, there is value in the interaction that flows from online teaching and learning, and in providing learners the opportunity to contribute more fully to the development of programmes by providing some of the content themselves then more sophisticated approaches pertain. However, these approaches require sophisticated appreciation of pedagogical approaches and are costly, and currently we have some way to go before we are to reduce costs substantially.

Notes

1 In the field of lifelong learning, for example, the University of Linkoping in Sweden offers together with universities from Australia, Canada and South Africa an Intercontinental Masters Programme in Adult Learning and Global Change (see http://www.ibv.liu.se/int_master/main_page.htm). At a European level, universities in Belfast, Kaunas, Lapland, Lund, Malta, Stirling and Tartu offer together an online Masters in Lifelong Learning and Regional Development (see http://www.ioe.stir.ac.uk/) and the Danish University of Education offers collaboratively with the Institute of Education in London a European Masters in Lifelong Learning: Policy and Management (see http:// www.lifelonglearningmasters.org).
2 We distinguish between these different forms of social capital in Chapter 3.
3 Phoenix University has become in a very short time one of the world's largest university offering programmes from Associate Degree to Doctoral level to some 200,000 students at almost 200 locations mainly in the US using both online and face-to-face delivery. Its main target group is working professionals. See http://www.phoenix.edu/
4 This site has been developed to give advice to teachers and students in the K-12 classroom in the US concerning strategies for videoconferencing and is accessible at http://www.d261.k12.id.us/VCing/index.htm. Many similar sites exist.
5 The UK Open University announced in October 2006 that its learning materials would be made freely accessible on the Internet to students and teachers, following the lead of other major universities such as MIT.
6 This is discussed further in Chapter 2.
7 The concept has gained more credibility than it may deserve and as Coffield *et al.* (2004) have pointed out, many of the claims made for individual preferences in learning and subsequent implications for teaching are founded on data gathered using methodologies that have inadequate levels of validity. The measurement of a preferred learning style is however immensely popular and used widely in education. Coffield *et al.*'s research identifies 71 models, 13 of which describe as major models and subsequently analyse in some depth.

References

Ahmed, A. and Nwagwu, W.E. (2006) Challenges and opportunities of e-learning networks in Africa. *Development,* 49(2): 86–92.

Allan, B. and Lewis, D. (2006) Virtual communities as a vehicle for workforce development: A case study. *Journal of Workplace Learning,* 18(6): 367–383.

Anderson, P. (2005) *Mobile and PDA Technologies: Looking around the Corner,* at http:// www.jisc.ac.uk/uploaded_documents/jisctsw_05_04pdf.pdf

Biggs, J.B. (1999) *Teaching for Quality Learning at University: What the Student Does.* Buckingham: Society for Research into Higher Education/Open University Press.

Candy, P.C. (1991) *Self-direction for Lifelong Learning. A Comprehensive Guide to Theory and Practice.* San Francisco: Jossey-Bass.

Coffield, F., Moseley, D., Hall, E. and Ecclestone, K. (2004) *Learning Styles and Pedagogy in Post-16 Learning: A Systematic and Critical Review*. London: Learning and Skills Development Agency, at http://www.lsda.org.uk/files/PDF/1543.pdf

European Commission (2001) The Memorandum on Lifelong Learning, at http://www.europa.eu.int/comm/education/life/index.html.

Ferlander, S. and Timms, D. (2001) Local nets and social capital, *Telematics and Informatics* 18(6): 51–65.

Gallacher J., Osborne M. and Cloonan M. (1999) *The Research Agenda in Lifelong Learning*. Glasgow/Stirling: Centre for Research in Lifelong Learning, at http://www.stir.ac.uk/ioe/crll.

Gorard, S. and Selwyn, N. (1999) Switching on the learning society? Questioning the role of technology in widening participation in lifelong learning. *Journal of Educational Policy* 14(5): 523–534.

Global Alliance for Information and Communication Technologies and Development (GAID) (2007) *Progress Report 2006*, at http://www.un-gaid.org/en/system/files/GAID+2006+progress+report.pdf

Hodgson, V. and Reynolds, M. (2005) 'Consensus, difference and "mulitple communities" in networked learning'. *Studies in Higher Education* 30(1): 1–24.

Hung, D.W.L. and Chen, D. (2001) Situated cognition, Vygotskian, thought and learning from the communities of practice perspective: Implications for the design of web-based e-learning. *International Council for Educational Media*, at http://www.tandf.co.uk/journals.

Illeris, K. (2002) *The Three Dimensions of Learning: Contemporary Learning Theory in the Tension Field between the Cognitive, the Emotional and the Social*. Leicester: NIACE.

Jonassen, D. (1998) Designing constructivist learning environments. In Reigeluth, C.M. (ed.) *Instructional Theories and Models*, 2nd Edition. Mahwah: Erlbaum.

Lave, J. and Wenger, E. (1991) *Situated Learning: Legitimate Peripheral Participation*. Cambridge: Cambridge University Press.

Mayes, J. (2002) *Pedagogy, Lifelong Learning and ICT*. A Discussion Paper for the IBM Chair presentation, 18 May 2000, at http://www.ipm.ucl.ac.be/ChaireIBM/Mayes.pdf

Moore, M.G. (1999) Institutional restructuring: Is distance education like retailing? *American Journal of Distance Education* 13(1): 1–7.

Pechey, B. (2006) Is video-conferencing set for take off? *IT Week*, 29 May 2006.

Postle, G. and Sturman, A. (2003) Widening access to higher education – An Australian case study. *Journal of Adult and Continuing Education*, 8(2): 195–218.

Postle, G., Sturman, A., Mangubhai, F., Cronk, P., Carmichael, A., McDonald, J., Reushle, S., Richardson, L. and Vickery, B. (2003) *Online Teaching and Learning in Higher Education: A Case Study*. Canberra: Department of Education, Training and Youth Affairs.

Taylor, J.C. (1996) *Technology, pedagogy and globalisation*. Keynote address presented at the UNESCO funded Asia-Pacific Workshop on Vocational Education and Distance Education, Korea Open University, Seoul, October.

Taylor, J.C. (2001) *Fifth generation distance education*. Keynote address, 20th ICDE World Conference, Dusseldorf, Germany 1–5 April.

Tennant, M. (1997) *Psychology and Adult Learning*, 2nd Edition. London: Routledge.

Tennant, M. (2006) Cognition. In Jarvis, P. and Parker, S. (eds) *Human Learning – An Holistic Approach*. London: Routledge, pp. 101–115.

Timms, D. (2007) Identity, local community and the Internet. In Osborne, M. Sankey, K. and Wilson, B. (eds) *Social Capital, Lifelong Learning and the Management of Place.* London: Routledge.

United Nations (2000) *United Nations Millennium Declaration.* New York; UN, at http://www.un.org/millennium/declaration/ares552e.htm

Vygotsky, L.S. (1978) *Mind in Society: The Development of Higher Psychological Processes.* Cambridge, MA: Harvard University Press.

Wellman, B. (2001) Physical place and cyberplace: The rise of networked individualism. In Keeble, L. and Loader, B.D. (eds) *Community Informatics: Shaping Computer-Mediated Social Relations.* London: Routledge.

Chapter 11

Conclusion

It was the best of times, it was the worst of times, it was the age of wisdom, it was the age of foolishness, it was the epoch of belief, it was the epoch of incredulity, it was the season of Light, it was the season of Darkness, it was the spring of hope, it was the winter of despair, we had everything before us, we had nothing before us, we were all going direct to Heaven, we were all going direct the other way – in short, the period was so far like the present period, that some of its noisiest authorities insisted on its being received, for good or for evil, in the superlative degree of comparison only.

(Dickens, 1985, 35)

Perhaps all generations believe that theirs is on the verge of, or responsible for, revolutionary change (perhaps they are). This sometimes means that we ignore stasis and emphasise change in the *superlative degree*. And the impulse to futurology is great – even for terminally cautious academics.[1] In the case of lifelong learning, it is difficult to avoid superlatives since the meanings or discourses, practices and institutions of 'lifelong learning' have already changed considerably in a relatively short period of time. What is immediately obvious in contemporary society is the ever widening scope of lifelong learning policies and practices. Lifelong learning is increasingly bound up with economic and social policies as well as educational policies. It encompasses new approaches to schooling and to community learning and increased participation is supported by virtual learning and learning in the workplace. It is pertinent to wonder to what extent the concept of lifelong learning will lose its meaning as institutions and practices continue to transform themselves. Patricia Cross in 1981 had already recognised the potential for blurring of meaning in this domain in quoting Richardson (1979) who had stated that ' "lifelong education" means anything you want it mean'.

However at this historical juncture, lifelong learning is profoundly implicated in particular economic and social changes and we suggested in the introduction that a useful way of thinking about lifelong learning is as a fluid strategy for change. It is partly a strategy that is applied by governments in policies and practices and is supported by supra-national organisations such as the OECD, UNESCO and the EU. However, it is also a set of discourses about individuals, communities, and the workplace and about the role of education and training. These discourses and new practices potentially create possibilities for greater participation in education and training in emancipatory ways. But they also place new responsibilities and constraints on individuals and potentially increase governmental influence and control over institutions, those who work in them and individual learners. It is therefore not surprising that lifelong learning is such a contested concept and that educationally we may appear to be living in both the 'best and worst of times'. Education has never been more at the heart of government policies. At the same time, institutional practices are under very considerable pressure to reform and we noted in the introduction that the reorganisation of education and training has been an important element of the journey towards the learning society. Here, we close our discussion of lifelong learning by briefly revisiting some selected themes from the chapters in this text. We have deliberately simplified trends in a somewhat dichotomous manner as a way of emphasising both possibilities and constraints.

Individualisation and connectivity

In educational discourses, the individual is increasingly placed at the centre of learning in both rhetoric and practice, for example, in discourses which emphasise learner-centredness, personalised learning, individual responsibility for learning (and employability), greater individual choice and the rights of 'consumer-learners'. Boshier (2001), for example, speaks of the 'autonomous free floating individual learner as consumer'. We argued in Chapter 2 that lifelong learning discourses and practices have the potential to reconstruct learner identities in ways that are adaptive to particular social and economic changes. Moreover, there is an ever increasing emphasis on the self in contemporary culture and pressures to participate in self-optimising practices of various kinds, including, of course, lifelong learning activities. These are potentially positive developments to the extent that they are enabling. However, we wish to reiterate some of our questions about the way in which individuals are able to resource these new identities.

The individualistic nature of lifelong learning discourses and contemporary culture (and some social theories) obscure issues of cultural and identity capital. This leads to individual deficit explanations for failure to participate in learning successfully. Skeggs (2004) has argued powerfully that identities are not simply available in equal measure to all for the choosing, thus underlining the social nature of identity. In other words, particular social groups may be more vulnerable to negative labelling. In addition, imperatives to act in a self-interested manner pose ethical challenges for individuals enmeshed in caring relations and potentially for teaching staff and for educational institutions. Lifelong learning discourses are extremely varied and, significantly, not linked to a particular framework of values. For example, they are capable of producing practices dedicated to an education-led economy as Young (1998) has called for, but equally well able to produce an economy-led education. The dilemmas around these new identities have the potential to create significant 'cognitive dissonance' and/or 'alienation' for all individuals engaged in competitive, performative and self-optimising milieux. These issues imply the need for critical reflexivity in engaging in lifelong learning on the part of learners and teachers and the challenges these issues pose should not be underestimated.

Paradoxically given this individualism, lifelong learning practices such as, distance learning, greater use of ICT in learning using rapidly developing virtual platforms, inter-agency working in learning regions, inter-institutional collaboration, portable credit, inter-agency working in community schools, partnership across public and private agencies in community learning, proposals to coordinate compulsory learning for 16–18-year-olds across a number of agencies and so on all require increased connectivity between providers of learning opportunities. They also have the potential to bring together communities of learners. There are a number of issues that could be highlighted here. In the case of learning communities or regions, the balance between the economic and the social aims would seem to be crucial in determining the nature of learner engagement and perhaps also the extent to which learning regions or cities are able to generate social capital and indeed, whether or not that social capital does in fact increase participation in learning. Successful inter-agency working and the nature of partnerships formed with communities of learners will be crucial in determining what kinds of learning communities emerge. As we noted in Chapter 8, there is concern that some interventions will undermine community self-determination. In the case of the potential of virtual learning, again, the quality of the virtual environment is important in determining the kind of learning community that emerges.

There is, however, a sense that in the enthusiasm for creating 'networks', forming partnerships and engaging in innovative practice that the question of what kind of learning community is being created is lost. In terms of virtual learning, there is still a problem of access for the lowest socio-economic groups even in the richest countries. We also have evidence, as we noted in Chapter 8, that in contemporary Britain individuals are more likely to engage in leisure pursuits that do not involve social interaction. This tendency may have implications for participation in virtual learning worlds, where dominant pedagogical approaches based around social constructivism with its emphasis on interaction, communication and co-construction may be at odds with the individualism encouraged in many other spheres of life. Moreover, it is clear that increasing numbers of people are participating in virtual worlds (and in many cases making 'non-virtual' money in them). Communities are continually being remade and lifelong learning practices are playing a part in this. It is therefore timely that we should be asking what sort of learning communities we are aiming for.

Acceleration and stasis

One significant aspect of inter-institutional connectivity is that of flexible provision, which potentially allows students greater choice in terms of when and where work is completed (as in distance learning), greater choice of institution and the potential to move between institutions and sectors more easily. The discursive aspects of flexibility have been critically explored by a number of authors (e.g. Crowther, 2004; Nicoll, 2006). However, the extent to which flexible participation also means acceleration of learning and therefore acceleration of the pace of life more generally is less discussed.[2] The assumption is that flexible arrangements free up space and time for participation in learning and this may indeed be the case given the time saved in not having to travel to classes. However, the benefits are likely to vary between social groups.

First, flexible working practices have a differential impact across social groups. At one end of the continuum, zero hours contracts and changing shift patterns are very restrictive and likely to make flexible participation in learning less easy (see Purcell, Hogarth and Simm, 1999 and Brendon et al., 1999) than individuals whose working practices allow them to choose their own hours and perhaps even use office facilities to log in and out of their virtual learning environment. Second, learners with significant domestic work and/or caring responsibilities may find the *lack* of spatial and temporal demarcations between learning and other activities difficult to manage – in addition to the simple lack of time they may experience. Unfortunately, flexible provision does not make time elastic. However, there is an assumption within discourses of flexibility that we can all do more things.[3] In this way, lifelong learning practices are implicated in the acceleration of the pace of life. This is potentially positive for those who value being able to do more things. Some might argue that those in lower socio-economic groups are not necessarily time poor.[4] However, the evidence on the impact of work would imply that these groups have less control over the time that is potentially available to them. The point here is that space and time do not disappear when students engage flexibly and the economics of time may be such that 'doing more things' is not an option for some learners especially at particular points in the life course such as forming a family. This potentially leaves some individuals in the 'slow lane'. These aspects of access to learning are sometimes obscured in the somewhat excitable discussion of hyper-mobility, multi tasking and time-space compression which characterises much academic discourse, which is why we raise them here.

Concluding remarks

One of the most dynamic aspects of lifelong learning policies and practices in recent years is the emergence of a changing balance between economic and social concerns. This is evident in increasing governmental interest in the social benefits of learning such as the improved health outcomes associated with increased length of education, the interest in social capital theories in the academic and policy communities, an increasing interest in informal learning and in new approaches to working with communities. This may be, as Schuller, Baron and Field (2000, 13) have argued *a revalorization of social relationships in political discourse*. However, it could also be the case that lifelong learning is increasingly seen as the answer to perceived social problems – for example as in the call for education for parents who are identified as 'inadequate', which raises the issue of increasing governmentality. The renewed concern with social aspects of learning and a social problem orientation are not of course necessarily contradictory. However, there may be differences of approach and differences in the extent to which participants are able to choose whether or not to participate and hence to be able to determine content and outcomes. A revalorisation of the social implies a return to questions of social and economic inequalities. While lifelong learning may not – to paraphrase Bernstein – be able to compensate for society, an enormous amount of effort has already been expended in widening access to learning to previously excluded groups. But this has proved an extremely intransigent problem. One of the hopes for the development of policy and practice in lifelong learning is that the renewed interest in the social dimensions of learning will bring some success in tackling extremely entrenched educational inequalities.

Notes

1 Less cautious is an editorial by Carneiro (2007) and subsequent articles in the *European Journal of Education*, Volume 42(2). These provide some speculations of future scenarios for learning based on discussions held at two fora of the International Futures Forum (see http://www.internationalfuturesforum.com/projects.php?id=4). De Boer and Westerheijden (2005) provide a good account in the context of HE of the creating of future scenario planning based on the Delphi method, the outputs of which we quote at the end of Chapter 6.
2 However, see Usher and Edwards (2007) Chapter 2 for a summary of perspectives on speed and fast capitalism.
3 Thrift (1999) contends that this is specific to Anglo-American culture. He goes on to argue that while the nineteenth and twentieth centuries were characterised by spatial colonialism, the twenty-first century is increasingly characterised by colonisation of the temporal. This implies an accelerated pace of life.
4 We would not. See Ehrenreich and Hoschild (2003) and Hochschild (1997) for a discussion of the way in which the wealthy are able to defend and increase the time available to them.

References

Boshier, R.W. (2001) Lifelong learning as bungy jumping: In New Zealand what goes down doesn't always come up. *International Journal of Lifelong Education* 20(5): 361–377.

Brendon, J.B. et al. (1999) *Job Insecurity and Work Intensification: Flexibility and the Changing Boundaries of Work.* York: Joseph Rowntree.

Carneiro, R. (2007) The Big Picture: Understanding learning and meta-learning challenges. *European Journal of Education* 42(2): 152–171.

Cross, K.P. (1981) *Adults as Learners: Increasing Participation and Facilitating Learning.* San Francisco: Jossey Bass.

Crowther, J. (2004) 'In and against' lifelong learning: Flexibility and the corrosion of character. *International Journal of Lifelong Education* 23(2): 125–136.

De Boer, H. and Westerheijden, D. (2005) Scenarios as a method. In Enders, J., File, J., Huisman, J. and Westerheijden, D.F. (eds) *The European Higher Education and Research Landscape 2020: Scenarios and Strategic Debates*. Enschede: Center for Higher Education and Policy Studies (CHEPS), athttp://www.utwente.nl/cheps/publications/downloadable_publications/downloadablesenglish.doc/

Dickens, C. (1985) Introduction. In George Woodcock (ed.) *A Tale of Two Cities*, Illustrations by Hablot K. Browne. London: Penguin.

Ehrenreich, B. and Hochschild, A. (2003) *Global Woman, Nannies, Maids and Sex Workers in the New Economy*. London: Granta.

Hochschild, A. (1997) *Time Bind: When Work Becomes Home and Home Becomes Work*. New York: Metropolitan Books.

Nicoll, K. (2006) *Flexibility and Lifelong Learning: Policy, Discourse and Politics*. London: Routledge.

Purcell, K., Hogarth, T. and Simm, C. (1999) *Whose Flexibility? The Costs and Benefits of 'Non-standard' Working Arrangements and Contractual Relations*. York: Joseph Rowntree.

Richardson, P.L. (1979) *Lifelong Education and Politics in Policies for Lifelong Education*. Washington DC: American Association of Community and Junior Colleges.

Schuller, T., Baron, S. and Field, J. (2000) Social capital: A review and critique. In Baron, S., Field, J. and Schuller, T. (eds) *Social Capital Critical Perspectives*. Oxford: Oxford University Press.

Skeggs, B. (2004) *Class, Self, Culture*. London: Routledge.

Thrift, N. (1999) The place of complexity. *Theory Culture and Society* 16(3): 31–69.

Usher, R. and Edwards, R. (2007) *Lifelong Learning – Signs, Discourses, Practices*. Dordrecht: Springer.

Young, M.F.D. (1998) *The Curriculum of the Future: From the 'New Sociology of Education' to a Critical Theory of Learning*. London: Falmer Press.

Index